"BLESSED ARE YE"

BLESSED ARE YE:
TALKS ON THE BEATITUDES
By F. B. MEYER, B.A.

Published at 57 & 59 Ludgate Hill
By the Sunday School Union
London . . . . MDCCCXCVIII

FIRST EDITION printed . . *September* 1898

Reprinted . . . . . *November* 1898

PREFACE

IT was, so the Evangelist tells us, from the mountain slopes above Capernaum, that our Lord delivered the sermon, of which the Beatitudes form the noble and sublime introduction.

Now, it is with mountains that we are wont to associate far-reaching views which stretch to the golden horizon, and the streams which descend, with musical roar, to water the plains.

In these respects, how remarkable the resemblance between this Octave of Blessedness, and the mountain on which the Lord was sitting, when these gracious words proceeded from his mouth!

For sublimity, for comprehensiveness, and for power of enriching the lowlands of human life, it is hard to find a parallel even in His words.

It is impossible to exhaust them. The maturing experience of Christian manhood is as unable to explore all their wealth of meaning as the open-eyed wonder of the young disciple. And the simple purpose of this booklet is to show some of the pathways that conduct into the heart of these mountains of God.

F. B. MEYER.

CONTENTS

"BLESSED ARE YE"

I

THE EIGHT GATES INTO THE CITY OF BLESSEDNESS

AFTER a year's ministry in Judæa, the records of which are scanty, the Lord Jesus went down to inaugurate His public ministry in Galilee. Rejected, because of the Bethesda miracle, by the Scribes and Pharisees, He threw Himself on the masses of the people. Threatened with death, He took steps to make His kingdom permanent by gathering around Him His closest friends, and by selecting from them twelve to be with Him, and to go forth to preach the glad tidings of the Gospel of Peace.

The night before the morning, which was to be

thus signalised, was spent by Him in prayer. He assured Himself, during those lone dark hours, more fully of His Father's purpose; received definitely at the Father's hands those that had been His, but who were now to be transferred to Himself; asked with a new tenderness that they might be worthy of their high calling as the foundation stones of the New Jerusalem. Thus He girded Himself beneath the quiet stars for what awaited Him on the morrow.

As the dawn broke He called unto Him whom He would. The band of the disciples furnished those who were now chosen apostles. From those who had been attracted to Him by His marvellous personality, as well as by the indication of the Baptist, He selected the twelve who were summoned to be foremost in peril and temptation, as they were to be nearest and closest in sympathy and friendship.

Finally, with these beside Him, He descended the mountain slope to a little level place, where a vast crowd awaited Him, gathered from the whole surrounding country, and beseeching His miraculous healing for their sick. "And he healed them." Then the multitudes settled down to hear this marvellous discourse, the inauguration of His kingdom, the unfolding of His Galilean ministry. It was a great occasion. Below, the lake; above, the morning sky; around, the hills, on the flanks of which lay long lines of fleecy cloud; the air fragrant with the scent of flowers and new-mown grass, and thrilling with the expectation of the expectant throng. The newly-healed and their bearers, friends and critics, apostles and disciples, hanging on those lips that spake as never man spake.

This was the Sinai of the New Dispensation.

But how great the contrasts!

Moses was a servant; here the Son.

Moses spake amid the peal of thunder and the quivering of the earth; here it was a perfect spring morning, and the only sounds were those of nature, or the murmur of the towns below stealing around.

Moses bore ten awful words, graven on granite tables; but these were gentle, tender words, written on fleshly tablets of the heart.

Moses was storm-girt and terrible; but grace and truth came by this wondrous Man, whose words reach down to the weakest, humblest, weariest.

Moses spake of the curse; but He opened His mouth, and taught them, saying, Blessed.

It was meet that the Master should open His public ministry with beatitudes.—It was thus He finished it. "It came to pass, while He blessed them, He parted from them, and was carried up into heaven." His last words bent back again to His first words, as in a bridal ring; and all were goldened with the radiance of eternity. And since He has been hidden from our gaze, unseen though loved, His voice from out the throne has spoken many a beatitude beside, recorded for us in the Book of Revelation. How ill do they understand our Master, who fear Him as hard and austere. He is inspired by motives of the purest benevolence; and if He use the knife it is only to cut away what conflicts with our purest bliss, and of which we would be eager to be relieved, if we knew, as certainly as He, what makes for our peace.

> "His every act pure blessing is,
> His path, unsullied light."

Blessedness is the attitude of Deity.—Before Jesus came men were content, or happy, or mad with hilarious excitement, but not really blessed. This

was a new word for them, or it was an old word,
new minted. They knew nothing of this deep
sweet secret of enjoying even in this world something of the very life of the Deity. No climber
had as yet made his way to the lake that lay far
up among the hills, mirroring Infinity and Eternity
in its pellucid surface. Only He who had come
down from heaven, and during His earthly ministry
was in heaven, knew of its existence, or of the path
that led to it.

God is significantly called "the Blessed God."
From all eternity, His vast and glorious nature has
been as blessed as the vault of heaven seems full
of ether. And Jesus came down from heaven to
discover to us this fact, and to make us understand
our privilege. Since we have been made in the
likeness of God, we are capable, each one, of a
similar blessedness. One spirit with the Lord, we
are privileged to share the very blessedness that
fills His heart. Not in quantity, but in quality ;
not in measure, but in essence, we may know what
the blessedness of the blessed God is.

It is for us now and here.—Not away in some
distant world of bliss, where our circumstances
shall be entirely favourable, and the mystery of

sin and death ended, but in whatsoever situation
we may be found at this present hour. Our real
troubles are not in our circumstances, but in ourselves; and there have been thousands who, in
precisely those straits which now cost us such
anguish, have been deeply and infinitely blessed.
If we had lived Paul's life, in our present state of
heart, we should have known nothing of his
rapturous experiences; and if he could live in ours
to-day, however tempest-tost and troubled, he
would find in it the elements of such exceeding
rapture, that whether in the body or out of it, he
would not be able to tell.

Jesus came to show that blessedness did not
consist in our outward environment. Indeed, He
distinctly taught that we might expect to suffer
additional distresses for His and righteousness'
sake. But amidst all He was intent on teaching
that, if we possessed certain moods and were
animated by a certain temper, we might be truly
blessed. He shows in these matchless words that
blessedness is possible in the saddest lives, if only
we will bear ourselves simply, bravely, truly,
purely. Blessed are the poor in spirit. . . . Blessed
are they that have been persecuted for righteous-

ness' sake : for theirs is the kingdom of heaven (Matt. v. 10).

This blessedness is for all.—These waters run in the valley, accessible to the rootlets of the tiniest flower, and to the cup of the child. I used to think that God had put His best gifts on a high shelf for us to reach up to them. I now find that the best are on the lowest shelves, on the level of the nursery floor, that the babes may get them. There is a capacity for blessedness in each and all, just as there is a capacity for beauty, for love, for joy. The water of the well of Bethlehem was for David alone, but the water of the deep well of God's bliss, which our mighty Saviour has won for us at awful cost, is for each poor outcast who comes, pitcher in hand, to take it freely.

There is no respect of persons with God. He does not exclude any, He welcomes all. Whosoever thou art, thou art bidden to this feast; thou mayest eat angels' food; thou mayest be blessed in thy poor measure, as the Eternal God is in His ; thou mayest be ever with Him, and all that He has be thine. Sunshine and wild flowers are for village children equally as for the sons of peers; and the blessedness which thrills the holy ones within the vail, may shed its glow and fragrance on thy heart also.

There are eight doors into the blessed life.—Like the gates of the New Jerusalem, they stand open day and night; and one, at least, faces each of us. We have but to walk out of ourselves and into that open doorway, and so into the blessed life. It is impossible to be a Christian and not within easy reach of one of these open doors, because if we cannot lay claim to purity, meekness, or merciful-ness, we can at least class ourselves among those that hunger and thirst after righteousness, and long to be filled; or among those who, in their deep consciousness of poverty, count themselves to have no part or lot in the matter; or among those that mourn, because they cannot mourn enough, and beat their breasts because they cannot weep purer and more unselfish tears.

Thou art not pure in heart: then that door into blessedness is blocked against thee; but thou art sore sorrowful that thou art not pure : then go into the kingdom through the door of mourning and contrition.

Thou art not meek, thy proud spirit frets within thee, never prouder than when assuming the garb of humility, not to be outdone by others in pretensions to holiness; but thou art consumed by a hunger for righteousness, which refuses to be satisfied, then pass in through *that* door and be blessed.

Eight is an octave ; and is the number of resurrection. —Seven speaks of a completed work, as at the creation, but eight introduces a new week. It was on the eighth day that Jesus rose from the dead. Blessedness is possible only to those who have passed into the resurrection life, because to them only is opened the possibility of attaining to those properties of spirit which have been indicated.

It is not enough to look to Jesus on the cross as our Substitute, we must be identified with Him as our Head, and realise that, through our union with Him, we have been transferred to " the heavenlies," where He lives and reigns with the Father and the Holy Ghost. We must belong, by spiritual affinity, to the age of Pentecost. We must know the in-filling and anointing of the Holy One. We must accept the death of Christ, as isolating us from the life of worldliness and fleshliness, and introducing us into the power and grace of the Divine Spirit.

2

When this is fully realised, and Christ is formed within us by the operation of the Holy Ghost, we shall become conscious of the uprising within, like the slender snowdrops through the hard mould of winter, of those dispositions which are the keys and doors to blessedness.

Blessedness has many aspects.—It contains the promise of victory and supremacy: "theirs is the kingdom." It breathes comfort over the troubled and perplexed: "they shall be comforted." It gives the earth as a heritage, so that all things become the property of the soul which is united with God. It satisfies and fills. It strews life's pathway with the mercy of man as well as of God. It involves the faculty of vision. It stamps its possessor as a child of the Highest. It sheds the oil of joy on the head, and casts the mantle of praise over the spirit of heaviness. Such are the creeks, bays, and inlets of that inland sea.

All these may be thine. As each of the conditions tends to induce all the rest, so does each of the rewards pass ultimately into the possession of the obedient and believing soul. Poverty of spirit leads to mourning, and this to meekness, and this to an inappeasable hunger, and this to mercifulness, and this to purity of heart, and this to peace-making. Similarly, we begin and end with the kingdom of heaven—that is, our experience climbs upward as a spiral, and ends where it began, only in a fuller and richer experience. It is the same day, but there is a difference between the light of the meridian and of dawn. But between these two experiences of the kingdom lie comfort, possession, filling, mercy, vision, peace, and joy, and the one inevitably unfolds into another, as one hour into the next in the upward climbing of the sun.

Christ reverses men's most cherished notions.—But lately I stood beside a lake, in whose calm waters, as they lapped the shore, I saw the foliage of the brake, which fringed the margin, reflected. But everything was reversed. What was highest on the land was deepest in the water, what was lowest on the land was highest in the water. The tree-tops lay fathoms deep, the daisies and anemones were close at hand; and I saw that this was a parallel of what is happening around. What is much esteemed by man is reckoned little of in the estimate of eternity. The gold for which we strive, and on which we count, is employed to make

the pavement of the New Jerusalem. Whilst
the humility which washes disciples' feet, the
meekness which takes an insult quietly, are the
royal and leading features of that heavenly world.
The King rides on an ass, and an ass's foal. Of
the pride, and circumstance, and power, which
men put first, Christ makes nought; of the
meekness and humility, which men despise,
Christ makes all. He lifts poverty out of the
dunghill, and makes it sit among the princes of
the heavenly realm; and Mordecai is exalted
above Haman.

*Christ realised the characteristics and blessedness of
which He spoke* —He was poor in spirit, and classed
Himself among the babes: our King was meek
and lowly of heart; He hungered after God, and
spent the nights in endeavouring to appease His
hunger; so merciful that publicans and sinners
were attracted to Him; so pure that He always
beheld the Father's presence; ever making peace,
and incessantly persecuted. Oh, lovely pattern of
all Thou didst inculcate! All unconsciously Thou
wast limning Thyself in these sentences.

His, too, was this blessedness. Storms of evil-
speaking and evil-doing might assail Him; but

deep in His heart the life of God lay warm, as nature hides the secret of the coming year deep in her breast, whilst wintry storms sweep over the sky.

Listen to Him; learn of Him; be like Him; receive Him into thine heart; let Him be revealed within thee, so shalt thou also be conformed to these qualities, and participate in this bliss.

Most Blessed Christ! Those whom Thou dost bless, are blessed indeed; lead me, I beseech Thee, by Thy good Spirit, into the enjoyment of these blessings which Thou hast prepared for them that love Thee, and which pass the mind of man to conceive.

II

THE KEY TO THE KINGDOM

" Blessed are the poor in spirit, for theirs is the kingdom of heaven."—MATT. v. 3.

HAD Salome and her sons remembered this beatitude, they would never have asked Christ to make them sit, one on His right, and the other on His left in His kingdom. They would have seen that it was not for Christ to give thrones by an act of His royal prerogative, but that places of power were conditioned by the preparation of heart in those who aspired to hold them. The throne is given to those for whom it is prepared; but they must previously have been prepared, and the preparation of heart involves the poverty in spirit from which the golden ladder of beatitudes climbs upward to blessedness.

Earthly thrones are generally built with steps up to them; the remarkable thing about the thrones of the eternal kingdom is that the steps are all down to them. We must descend if we would reign, stoop if we would rise, gird ourselves to wash the feet of the disciples as a common slave in order to share the royalty of our Divine Master.

WHAT IS THIS POVERTY OF SPIRIT?

1. *We must distinguish between poverty of spirit, and mean-spiritedness.*—None so poor in spirit as Jesus, yet, in all His bearing, with Pharisee, and Scribe, and Sanhedrin, there was an heroic bearing, a strength and intrepidity of spirit, a royalty of mien, which filled them with astonishment, and compelled the involuntary homage of his foes. "Behold a man!" said Pilate, as He came forth from the cruel scourging which was enough to take the manhood out of its victims, but in this case had left His majesty undiminished. "Per-

ceive ye not," said the Pharisees among themselves, "how we prevail nothing? Behold, the
world is gone after Him." And this trait has
always characterised the followers of Christ.
They have counted themselves poor, weak, the
offscouring of all things, but they have never
been deficient in those brave, strong, nobler
qualities of the soul which have enabled them to
stand unmoved amid the hatred of their fellows,
as some gaunt rock amid the ceaseless buffeting of
the waves.

2. *We must distinguish between poverty of spirit
and circumstances.*—Many have turned away from
what is fair and beautiful and right in nature, art,
intellectual attainment, and the acquisition of
property. They have said to themselves, Let us
fling away the wealth and treasure of our life, so
shall we be poor in spirit. But, surely, a man
may strip himself of all his belonging; his heart
atrophied for want of objects to love; his mind
wasting for want of knowledge; his imagination starved for want of nourishment; his life
shortened for want of the necessaries of physical
existence, and yet he may be as far as possible
from true poverty of spirit.

"Bethink Thee, Lord, while Thou and all the saints
Enjoy themselves in heaven; and men on earth
House in the shade of comfortable roofs,
Sit with their wives by fires, eat wholesome food,
And wear warm clothes, and even beasts have stalls,
I, 'tween the spring and downfall of the light,
Bow down one thousand and two hundred times
To Christ, the Virgin Mother, and the saints;
Or in the night, after a little sleep,
I wake; the chill stars sparkle; I am wet
With drenching dews, or stiff with crackling frost,
I wear an undrest goat-skin on my back;
A grazing iron collar grinds my neck;
And in my weak, lean arms, I lift the cross."

That is the boast of a man who has failed to discriminate between the voluntary poverty of circumstances and the humility of the spirit. All through such a life, the proud self asserts its vehemence, demanding recognition, and bringing, not the blood of the Lamb, but the firstfruits of its toil. You may bestow all your goods to feed the poor, and give your body to be burned, and yet not come within a thousand miles of true poverty of spirit; whilst, on the other hand, you may be rich in this world's goods, your heart warm with human love, and your mind, "like storied windows richly dight," receiving the many-coloured light of truth, and yet

carry ever the poverty of spirit which is as much
the habit and girdle of the soul as the horsehair
tunic which some of the greatest of the popes have
worn next their skin beneath the splendid pontifical
attire.

3. *We must also distinguish between poverty of
spirit and self-depreciation.*—There are people, most
objectionable, as I think, who are always saying, I
am nothing and nobody.   They insist on taking the
back seats, and declaring that they are not worth
your notice.   And yet you feel that they are as
proud and desirous of the first places, as those who
in the Lord's parable took the best positions at the
feast.   Indeed, the pride that apes humility is more
detestable than that which casts off all disguise.
We sometimes act humbly because we are proud of
a reputation of humility.   We sit near the door
that we may have the pleasure of being asked to
the front.   We assume a seraphic smile when most
annoyed, because we are so eager to pass muster
with the saints.   Oh for the humility which does
not count itself humble ! for the face which shines
and we wist it not ! for the simplicity of the little
child that does not turn back with admiration on
itself !

For true poverty of spirit we must turn to our blessed Lord, who, though He was rich, yet, for our sakes, became poor. In His case the spring of his action was altogether outside His own lovely and glorious nature, and was found in His Father. He did not forego the use of marvellous power, or the flow of unrivalled language, or that wealth of a noble nature with which He was endowed by the very constitution of His being. But all was held subservient to the will of His Father. No ambition lured Him forward, no fear held him back, no desire to win power apart from the paths marked out by the Father was allowed to divert Him from the chosen track of obedience. May we dare to say that Christ as man denied the exercise of His Divine attributes, that He might speak the words the Father gave Him, do the works that the Father wrought through Him, and fulfil the plan of life which the Father unfolded step by step. In absolute poverty of spirit, He received from God the impulse, power, and grace of daily living.

Poverty of spirit, therefore, is probably indicated by two characteristics. It has no pride of possession, and it is unconscious of ability to meet the demands made on it by the exigencies of its ministry.

Poverty of spirit has no pride in its possessions.—At the beginning of the Christian life, we earnestly endeavour after the acquisition of certain virtues and graces. We have read of them, or seen them exemplified in others, until they have cast over us the spell of their fascination. We strive for them, and sometimes congratulate ourselves on their partial attainment. Surely, the soul says to itself, as it compares the present with the past, I am purer, humbler, gentler than I was! There is an arraying of the soul in treasures and jewels, as when the young girl takes from her drawer one ornament after another, which has been given by admirers and friends. Full often this self-complacency is shattered by some terrible fall, or by repeated failure, till we come to see that we have no more claim to possess goodness than a room to possess light. These things are not our own, but received from Jesus, and enjoyed only in proportion as we abide in Him, and He in us. I am not good, but Jesus is in me the source of goodness; I am not humble, but Jesus dwells within me, bringing every proud thought and imagination into captivity to Himself. I am not strong, but I receive Him who is made unto me wisdom, righteousness, sanctification, and redemption. In absolute dependence upon the Saviour for the constant supply of His own nature through the Holy Ghost, we exemplify that growing sense of need which is one of the sure signs of the humble and contrite heart which God will not despise.

Poverty of spirit is unconscious of ability to meet the demands made on it by the exigencies of its ministry.— Men come smitten by a great need. "I am in mental perplexity—explain my difficulty." "I am bound hand and foot by the devil—loose me." "I am needing more of the Holy Ghost — teach me." "My child is grievously vexed with a devil —deliver her." In reply the poor in spirit say, "We have nothing which will suffice for needs like yours. Silver and gold have we none, but there is one thing we can do, we can pray, we can put you in union with God, we are willing to become the channel through which God can meet your need."

Was not this precisely the attitude of the apostle who said, that he held the treasure of God in an earthen vessel; though sorrowful, he was always rejoicing; though poor, he made many rich; though he had nothing, yet he possessed all things?

How may We become Poor in Spirit?

First, never look on any virtue as inherent to your character, but attribute each gift and grace to the dower of the Almighty. Be content to be a branch. If the fruit hangs ripe and full, magnify the properties of the root to which it must be attributed. Live by the Son, as He by the Father. The light that shines on sea and shore might rather be credited to the earth which is made beautiful by it, than that any grace of the Christian character should be credited to you or me, as though it were in any sense our own. What hast thou that thou hast not received?

Secondly, contrast yourself not with those below you, but with God above. We are too prone to compare our white robes with the stained garments of others, rather than with those robes which were whiter than a fuller could white them.

Thirdly, look on all the good in your neighbours. There is much more than we sometimes suppose, even in those who do not profess to be religious. Look not every man on his own things, but on the things of others. Let each account the other better than himself. There may be reasons why others have fallen short of the highest attainment, which if they had operated in our case would have dragged us to a lower depth ; whilst, if others had had our advantage they would almost certainly have stood far in advance of anything that we have attained.

Fourthly, consider yourself a trustee of God for others, so that whenever any demand is made on you for help, teaching, deliverance, you may confess before God your utter incompetence, and humbly claim that He should pass through your hand the wealth of bread which the poor traveller, who has come to your house, craves.

AND WHAT IS THE KINGDOM OF HEAVEN?

When Jesus spoke—and the same holds still—the kingdom was in mystery. It had not been manifested, nor, indeed, will it be until our King, now in hiding, is crowned King of the world. It consists not in meat and drink, but in righteousness, joy, and peace in the Holy Ghost.

It is the synonym of dignity, for those who have

the kingdom must be the children of the King. They are sons, heirs of God the Father, joint-heirs with the King Himself.

It is the condition of great influence, for the kingdom of God means peace on earth, goodwill towards men. To our Lord, the throne meant a greater ability to bless men, and that is the only reason why men should desire to sit on the right or left of His throne. To seek the kingdom for purposes of ostentation, self-emolument, and pride, were a vain and worthless ambition, despicable and contemptible; but to desire it that men may be rightly influenced, that the laws of right and healthy living should be laid down and maintained, that the poor should be avenged, and the wronged vindicated, this were a purpose worthy of God Himself. This is why the poor in spirit long for the royalties of the kingdom!

Lastly, it is the equivalent of large wealth. A kingdom in liquidation is an anomaly. We are wont to associate with the ideal king wealth like that of Solomon, of whom it is said, that in his days silver was as stones, and cedars as sycamore trees, and that he exceeded all the kings of the earth in wealth. Abundance! Largeness! Un-

bounded resource! Inexhaustibleness! Such are
the words that characterise the ideal kingdom.
So in the spiritual life.

We find Madame Guyon saying:—"This vast-
ness, or enlargedness, which is not bounded by
anything, increases every day; so that my soul,
partaking of the qualities of her spouse, seems also
to partake of His immensity."

And Thomas à Kempis in the *Imitation*:—"They
that willingly and freely serve Me shall receive
grace for grace. And if heavenly grace and true
charity, there will be no envy, nor narrowness of
heart, neither will self-love busy itself. For
Divine Love overcometh all things, and enlargeth
all the powers of the soul."

This is very wonderful. "Not after the manner
of men." The soul which is ever seeking to
aggrandise itself, and augment its stores, will miss
the true royalty of life, the treasures by which men
are enriched. But he who in the utter abnegation
of the self-life shall cast himself as a broken and
emptied vessel before God, will learn to say with
Hannah—

"The bows of the mighty men are broken,
    And they that stumbled are girded with strength,

3

They that were full have hired out themselves for
    bread ;
And they that were hungry have rest.
The Lord raiseth up the poor out of the dust,
He lifteth up the needy from the dunghill,
To make them sit with princes,
And inherit the throne of glory."

Thou, O Lord, didst become poor that through
Thy poverty we might be made rich; enrich me,
I pray Thee, with this same poverty of spirit,
that I may be a joint heir with Thee in Thy
Kingdom.

III

THE SECRET OF COMFORT

" Blessed are they that mourn : for they shall be comforted."—
Matt. v. 4.

THE Son came out from the infinite blessedness
of God to give man the key to perfect
blessedness, not only in the life hereafter, but in
this, so that in human hearts, also, the tide might
rise, which is ever full in the heart of the Infinite
One. Blessedness is more than gladness, pleasure,
the rapture of possession—perhaps words cannot
define it—but the heart knows when it enters
upon its heritage.

The conditions of human life, which men
naturally dread, are shown by Jesus to be the
elements out of which blessedness becomes possible.

He goes carefully through the various experiences
to which our race is heir—our tears, poverty,
hunger, temptation, persecution—and shows that
these are the material out of which blessedness is
produced, as the moisture of the air is necessary
for the production of the glories of sunrise and
sunset.

So comprehensive and far-reaching is this beatitude, that attempts have been made to limit its
scope and diminish its range of blessing. Surely
those only can be meant who sorrow with a
godly sorrow that needs no repentance! It is
remarkable how persistently men have interposed
such reservations on the munificence and largeness
of God's gifts. They assure one another that God
cannot mean all He says, and that it will be a
profound mistake to trust too absolutely in his
assurances. But, in spite of it all, notice the calm
strength of these words, "Blessed are they that
mourn : for they shall be comforted." Surely it
means that every sorrow carries in itself a clue
to blessedness, and that there is no sorrow
for which there are not healing and help in
the Gospel of Christ. In this soil grow all the
herbs which are suitable for the healing of

broken hearts. For all mourning He has the oil
of joy; for every heavy-laden spirit a garment of
praise.

Let no mourner turn away from these words, as
though they meant all else but him; and were too
wonderful, too rare, for those to participate in
whose sorrow is ordinary and common. Like all
the blessings of the gospel, they are for *whosoever
will*. They may be safely trusted to the uttermost.
Whoever thou art, and whatever the awful sorrow
which is gnawing at thine heart, thou shalt be
comforted. The seed of a harvest of blessedness
is hidden in these dark pods. An eternal weight
of glory is within thy reach, which will make thy
present affliction, when reviewed from the distant
future, seem light in comparison. Even though,
till now, thou hast not professed thyself a Christian,
thy grief may be the means of leading thee to the
source of everlasting consolation. Only do not
wrap thyself around with the heavy garments of
proud disappointment, do not shut thyself up alone
with thy grief, do not let it harden and corrode
thee, but humble thyself under the mighty hand
of God.

There are Five Fountains of Tears.

That opened by bereavement.—Sometimes the blow is sudden and unexpected; we had no idea that that light farewell was to be the last, and that the face would never turn back to give another sunny smile where the path passes out of sight. Sometimes the dear one fades as autumn leaves or the waning moon, visibly, gradually, inevitably. As long as there is life, we are too eager on its careful tending to give way to tears; but when all is over, in moments of reaction and despair, the fountains of the great deep are broken up. Then Rachel weeps for her children, and refuses to be comforted, because they are not; Martha and Mary weep to heart-break at their brother's grave.

For such there is comfort. Not in talking about change or diversion; not in platitudes about the common lot of man; not in invoking Time to festoon the ruin by hanging drapery of flowers and creeping plants; but by opening the heart to God, that He may instil, first by drops, then by slender rills, and afterwards by torrents, His

own blessed peace. It is God that the bereaved
soul needs most of all; and if bereavement
leads to Him; if the soul, deprived of its
natural support and comfort, turns its thought
and desire to the infinite light; if it is led
to feel the futility and failure of all that earth
can give, and seeks the treasures which are
hidden in the hand of God for all who come
for them; if the spirit, in its brokenness, seeks
the tender touch of the Good Physician for its
wounds and bruises, then comfort will arise, the
Comforter will come, Jesus will say, "I am glad
for your sakes I was not there, to the intent
that ye may believe."

The face is the mirror of the heart, and how
often in the calm, gentle look on the countenance,
the reposeful manner, the tender thoughtfulness
for others, which characterise those whose life
has been bereft of its light and joy, we recognise
that this beatitude has been fulfilled. "Blessed
are they that mourn: for they shall be comforted."
Not in the full life, but in the emptied one; not
in the sunny path, but in the shadowed one; not
in the house dight for the wedding, but in that
where darkened attire and subdued undertones

tell of recent sorrow, will you find that rare
plant growing most prolifically, which Jesus called
blessedness.

That opened by care and disappointment.—We
enter life with such high hope. Not more
gay is the colt, careering across the field, startled
by the scream of the engine and the rush of
the train of carriages! How soon are we caught,
and curbed, and put to the collar! Can it be
that the lightheartedness, the spring, the absence
of care, are for ever ended? Ideals blurred and
disappointed, years eaten with the canker-worm,
sunny mornings overcast by thick clouds! Poverty
in circumstance, feebleness of health, disappointment in love, the heart bereft of love, the spirit
broken by harsh tyranny, the constant limitation of
small means, dread of the pauper's dole. How
countless are the ills to which we are subject in
this world! From how many sources are the salt
drops contributed to the brine of the ocean of
grief! But Christ says that blessedness may be
found even here.

There are compensations in grief, and care, and
disappointment. How many have confessed that
they had never known the love of God, if human

love had not disappointed them; had never found the true riches, unless they had lost the heaped-up stores on which their hearts were fixed; had never realised the meaning of the Eternal and Divine, till the transience and vanity of earthly things were no longer the text of the preacher, but the experience of the heart? It is in moments of heart-break at the failure of all our hopes, that the Interpreter comes near to show unto man what is right for him. Then God is gracious unto him, and is heard saying, "Deliver from going down into the pit, let his life behold the light." Life without pain and trial is like a Chinese picture, with no depth or shadow.

That opened by the undertones of life.—Even in lives which do not share in the causes of grief already mentioned there is a dark undercurrent, a sense of sadness, and oppressive melancholy. Low and plaintive chords hide in every instrument, subtly underlie the most rapturous outbursts, and perhaps touch us more than they. There are shady, lonely, forbidding spots, the lairs of fever and malaria, in the loveliest woods, on the fairest summer days; expressions of unrest and dissatisfaction cross the sunniest faces; wailing notes sweep over every harp strung by earth's poets. "Vanity of vanities, all is vanity." It is the old complaint, and as true as it is old.

But this is well. There may be blessedness here. The heart of man must have some bitters in the cup of life, or he would drain it to intoxication and death. There must be freckle in the leaf, and stain on the flower, or man would forget that they were made to fade.

> "I thank Thee more that all our joy
> Is touched with pain ;
> That shadows fall on brightest hours ;
> That thorns remain ;
> So that earth's bliss may be our guide,
> And not our chain."

Broken cisterns drive to the Fountain of living waters. The vanity of all discloses the conclusion of the whole matter. The creaking tree impels the bird to build in the clefts of the rock.

That opened by sorrow for sin.—This is the work of the Spirit of God. Trouble may make us rebellious, passionate, hard ; but when the Spirit of God comes to us, already broken and crushed by trouble, and speaks to us of the love of God,

of the ideals we have missed, of the stains and
rents with which we have defiled our robes, of
the hurt we have done to those entrusted to us
for our succour and comfort, of the tears we have
caused to flow, of the stumbling-blocks we have
cast before the weak, of the talents we have
buried, of the thorns we have sown, tears of
godly sorrow flow freely, and of these there is
no need to repent. Let man's heart be brought
by the Spirit of God under the cross, and in
contact with the broken heart of Christ; let us
look on Him whom we pierced; let us realise
what sin is in the sight of the love and grief of
God, and the strongest will battle in vain with
the tears that rise unbidden to the eyes. But
each tear is the seed-germ of blessedness. Blessed
mourning this !

It is better to mourn for sin than for its consequences. It is not difficult to do the latter.
When we are reaping the bitter penalty of
mistake and crime, it is easy to be regretful.
"Oh, that I had not done this ! Would that I
had been more thoughtful and careful ! Might
I but have my chance again ! " So we all exclaim
often enough. But this is not sorrow for sin. That

is a deeper, nobler mourning far. Its tears are purer. In it is no taint of selfishness or dread of penalty. The convicted sinner weeps with unfeigned anguish, as he sees what his sin has meant to God, to Divine love and human, to those who have passed beyond his recall, or must for ever be influenced for the worse by his irrevocable past. And God carefully gathers up these tears, puts them in His bottle, writes them in His book.

That opened by the anguish of the world.—No true man can witness this unmoved. Every breath of air is laden with cries and sighings and prayers for help. "The whole world groaneth and travaileth together in pain." Children in an agony of fear beneath the heavy hand of drunken mothers and fathers; women wronged, maltreated, deserted; young hearts thrust relentlessly back from those whom they had been wont to count true; the slave in the Arabian dhow, the Armenian subjected to nameless indignity and torture, the cancer-ward, the madhouse, the torture-chamber of disease— Ah, my God, my very soul writhes as I write, when wilt Thou bring this scene of woe to an end! how long ere Thou dost arise to say that there shall be no more delay!

But it is blessed to mourn thus, for they that share with Christ in His griefs for men shall share His triumph when He sees of the travail of His soul and is satisfied; when He shall have destroyed the works of the Devil, and put down all rule, authority, and power. And even now there is blessedness in arising to relieve, so far as we can, the sorrow around us, for it is in helping others that we cease to brood over our own misfortunes, it is in wiping the tears of men that we forget to weep.

All that brings us in contact with the Man of sorrows, and acquaints us with His grief, is wholesome and blessed. If you would know Jesus, you must find Him, where Jairus is weeping over his daughter, and the widow is following her boy to the grave, in the porches of Bethesda and the dark shadows of Gethsemane, and such sorrow as we have been describing takes us there.

How bravely and nobly does Christ speak. All others sit as still in the presence of uncontrollable sorrow as Job's comforters did; or they endeavour, with well-meant words, to divert the troubled heart from its sources of anguish, but he says, do not

be afraid of sorrow, or evade it, or count it as a
wilderness; face it; bow yourself under the
mighty hand of God; look up into His face, and
believe that all has been permitted with the
tenderest purpose; ask Him to tell you His secret:
trust Him through all: out of the wrestle of the
dark night will come the salutation of the Prince
at the break of day.

In the judgment of Christ there is no grief that
cannot be consoled, no mourner that cannot be
comforted, no woe out of which the oil of joy
cannot be extracted.   Let us dare believe this, and
turn to Him, though our faces be wet with tears,
and our backs torn and bleeding, believing that
He has balm enough, anodynes and cordials, to
turn the shadow of death into the morning.

THESE ARE THE CONSOLATIONS OF CHRIST.

A sense of the love of God, that it is in, around,
over, and beneath us; always and everywhere; in
every circumstance, glad or sorrowful; in every
experience, patent to the world, or hidden in our
hearts.

The secret of humility, which resigns itself to the circumstances of life, because it has learnt to trace them, either to the appointment, or permission, of a love that cannot err, or be unkind.

The realisation of the unseen and eternal, which encompasses our little life, as the blue ether does our world, dipping into its valleys, lying about its mountains, and encompassing its path.

The presence of the Comforter.—" I will send Him unto you," the Master said. How vast the change He wrought. Before He came, the disciples were benumbed in hopeless grief. Paralysed with pain, they sat crushed and hopeless in the upper room till the glad hour, when Jesus was revealed as risen, living, glorified, by the blessed Paraclete. Then their sorrow was turned into joy; and there was fulfilled the Saviour's assurance that He would see them again, and their hearts should be glad, and their joy none should take away. It is from the darkness of the pit that men see the stars; and in the darkness of sorrow we behold the face of Christ, revealed by the Holy Spirit.

The hope of Heaven.—There we shall meet again the beloved and sainted dead; whilst tears will be wiped from off all faces by the hand of God. The

adversities and pangs of earth submerged in the
exceeding joy. All sin, and failure, and short-
coming for ever terminated. The mystery of evil
explained; the entail of sin ended: Death and
Hades cast into the Lake of Fire: whilst—

> Truth, and peace, and love, shall ever shine
> About the supreme throne
> Of Him, in whose happy-making sight alone,
> When once our heavenly-guided soul shall climb,
> Then all this earthly grossness quit,
> Attired with stars, we shall for ever sit
> Triumphing over death, and chance, and thee, O Time.

O Thou, who hast ascended on high that
Thou mightst give the Holy Spirit to comfort
us in all our sorrows and afflictions; impart
Him to me also, that I may be able to comfort
others with His tender consolations.

IV

THE HERITAGE OF THE EARTH

" Blessed are the meek: for they shall inherit the earth."—
MATT. v. 5.

THIS is the third regiment in the Lord's great
army, the third gate into the blessed life,
the third step downward to the throne. But what
sort of character is indicated? And how do the
meek differ from the poor in spirit?

There is evidently a distinction. The Lord said
that He was meek and lowly in heart (Matt. xi.
29); whilst the apostle plied his converts with
motives borrowed from the lowliness and meekness
of Christ (Eph. iv. 2). But what is that distinction?
The key to it is suggested by a passage from that
memorable last epistle, in which Paul the aged

4

gave his final instructions to the young Timothy, and especially as to his behaviour towards those who opposed themselves. "The servant of the Lord," he says, "must not strive; but be gentle unto all men, apt to teach, patient *in meekness,* instructing those that oppose themselves" (2 Tim. ii. 24, 25). Here *meekness* seems specially demanded, when we are summoned to meet the opponents of our faith or the traducers of our personal testimony.

May we not say, therefore, that poverty of spirit and lowliness of mind are one and the same thing, and denote the attitude of the spirit *towards God,* when conscious of the immeasurable distance between His majesty and its minuteness, His purity and its sinfulness; whilst meekness is the attitude of the spirit *towards men,* and especially towards the wrong of the world—to the evil that men perpetrate on each other, and especially on the saints of God?

Lowliness will always be a characteristic attribute of true saintliness. The very elders fall down before the throne, and cast their crowns at the feet of God in utter self-abasement. But, in heaven, though meekness will always shine with its mild ray in the prismatic band of perfection, there will be less room for its exercise, for those that oppose will have been taken out of the way, whilst the enemy and avenger will have been for ever stilled.

Meekness is consistent with strength of character.— It is not always thought so. Meekness is often used as a synonym for weakness, and meek people held in a considerable degree of contempt. There is no epithet that men of the world would more quickly and vehemently resent than the appellation "meek." A young officer would rather have a paving-stone hurled at him than this. A molluscous flabbiness, a contemptible namby-pambyism, an absence of backbone and muscle are the ideas which are generally summoned to our mind, when a man is classed among the meek.

Here, as so often, the superficial judgment of the world is falsified by a wide acquaintance with human character. Moses, the meekest of men, was the strong leader of the Jewish exodus, the Justinian of the Hebrew commonwealth, the Washington of the Jewish state. The meek Paul was as strong in bearing persecution, as he had formerly been in inflicting it, and stood like a rock against the insidious and persistent attempts of the Judaisers. His strong common sense laid the broad foundations of the Church in such wise that Jew and Gentile could meet as one. His strong intellect has laid the march of religious thought for eighteen centuries. And who shall say that Jesus Christ was not strong, viewing His nature only from the human side? Lamb though He was, He was the Lion of the tribe of Judah. The meekness with which He received the insults of His foes did not veil the strength which extorted the involuntary homage of Pilate. What strength to resist the soft seductions of the tempting voices that bade Him spare Himself! What strength to carry out the purpose of redemption, though He knew well all it would involve!

Man's misconception of this strength of meekness is largely due to the gentle guise which she adopts, the restraint which she exercises over herself, her soft footfall, her modulated tones. They do not pierce through the hiding of her power, and realise that there is even greater power required for the restraining of the manifestations of power, than in letting them have free play. It is a stronger thing for a man of vehement and impetuous temper to speak and act gently in the face of great provocation, than to blurt out indignant words and bluster like a north-east wind! The soft hand that restrains the fiery steed, is obviously as strong, and stronger. Ah! passionate souls, that pour out showers of glowing coals at every provocation, ye little know how evident is your weakness, where ye vaunt yourselves of strength, and how much more evident your strength would be if ye made the unruly passions within heed the strong sway of a steadfast purpose.

The meek man resists the incitement of personal resentment.—When wrong approaches us, it awakens two sentiments in our hearts, the one personal, the other more general; the first is the quickest and keenest, the other manifests itself generally after years of learning in the school of experience. It is natural for us to be stung to the quick by a feeling of resentment under rebuff, or slight, or rudeness, or wrong. It is, perhaps, rather an acquirement when men so identify their wrongs with the evil of the world that they pass from the consideration of personal indignity, absorbed by the view of the sea of tears and blood which is weltering round the world, visiting every shore, invading every home.

With the meek man this order is reversed. When wrong is done to him, he is led by the grace of God to mourn over it, as an indication of the misery of the soul that perpetrates the wrong, and of the great weight of injustice and tyranny beneath which the world groans. In other words, he suffers like a child of the Great Father; understands something of the anguish of God's heart in contact with the wrong of the world; leaves God to vindicate and avenge, and prays for the speedy coming of the day when all wrongs shall be righted, and tears wiped. The meek man joins his prayers with those of Christ, the supreme Sufferer, that the Father would forgive those who do more evil than they know.

The meek man is a quiet man.—The Apostle Peter beautifully joins these two virtues together when he says that women are not to seek their adornments in jewels or dress, but in the garb of the meek and quiet spirit. The meek spirit is quiet. It bears and suffers in silence. It does not retail

its wrongs, save in the ear of God, and then it does
not ask Him to requite, but to convert.   It weeps
more for the wrong-doer than for its wounds,
though they may bleed freely.   It anoints its
head, and washes its face, and appears not to men
to suffer.   Nipped by the sharp frost, it does not
waste regret over its tender shoots, but strikes its
roots deeper down into the dark loam of mother-
earth.   And out of this quiet confidence comes the
heroic strength which bears, believes, hopes, and
endures all things, till it conquers by the sheer
force of patience.   Nothing will so soon stop
cannon shot as sand.

The meek man rather bears wrong.—When the
apostle was urging his converts not to go to law
with one another, he said to them, " Why do ye
not rather take wrong ? "   What a mistake it is to
allow the passion that would do us harm to ignite
a kindred passion !   Let us understand that the
evil of speech and act which would injure us is set
on fire of hell, and nothing could better fulfil
the purpose of our great adversary than that the
passions should pass from the wrong-doer to the
wronged, and from him again to others.   When
the brazier is full of coals, and it is overturned so

as to ignite a house, we have an illustration of the
way in which a man whose soul is filled with
rancour, malice, and envy may spread his thoughts
and feelings. This is the great peril for us all.
Men of quick temper are extremely inflammable.
They are like touchwood to the flame, gunpowder
to the spark. The meek man, on the contrary,
meets wrong with a passive resistance which
quenches its fire; with a calm and gentle answer
he turns away wrath. With a resolute refusal to
be inflamed, he establishes a quarantine through
which the first germs of the epidemic cannot pass.
The spirit of meekness resembles the eucalyptus :
it is antiseptic, especially to the spread of passion.
If we could only surround every angry man with
a ring of meek souls, his passion would burn itself
out with comparative small damage.

*The meek man believes that the evil wrought to him
is permitted by God for wise purposes.*—As David
climbs Olivet, Shimei comes out to curse him.
Abishai urges to be allowed to still his vituperations
for ever, but the meek king says, "God hath said,
Curse David. Let him curse." In those strong
and bitter words David detected another voice, the
voice of One who loved him as a Father, whilst He

held his sin in utter detestation. Oh, it is well always to look for the appointment or permission of God! His appointment in the chastisement which comes in the course of providence, His permission in the stripes which come to us from the hands of the children of men. It is easy to be meek towards Judas and the mailed band when we can say, Shall I not drink the cup which my Father hath put into my hands?

The meek are marvellously guided.—" The meek will He guide in judgment : and the meek will He teach his way." The passionate soul is unable to detect the movements of God's guiding pillar. Passion raises a storm which blurs the heavens and ruffles the calm waters of the lake. In the eagerness with which the many waters of the soul argue and advise, the still small voice of the Divine Counsellor is drowned. When, therefore, you have been wronged, be calm and still. Wait for God. He will indicate the way He would have you take, the answer He would have you write, the acts of love with which you should retaliate.

The meek shall be vindicated.—It is foretold of the Messiah that He shall " reprove with equity for the meek of the earth." Not only hereafter, but now, is the judgment-seat set up, at which the oppressed plead their cause against their oppressors, and the Lord hearkens and hears. It is remarkable how perpetually wrongs perpetrated on the defenceless come back, like the boomerang of the savage, on their persecutors. Into the pit they dig they fall. Adonibezek cuts off the thumbs and toes of seventy kings, and his own are cut off. The Jews crucify Jesus of Nazareth, and so many of them are crucified by the Romans that wood fails for the crosses. The Rover sinks the Inchcape bell, and perishes on the rock from which it tolled.

The meek shall inherit the earth.—Even now the meek soul gets the best out of life. The world does not think so. It thinks that the meek must be worsted because they will not stand upon their rights, nor wield the sword in self-defence, nor meet men on their own terms. But, as ever, Christ's words stand the test of experience. The meek find more pleasure in simple joys than wrong-doers in all their wealth. Pure hearts find wells of peace and bliss in common sights and sounds. There is no twinge of conscience or bitter memory of wrong-doing to jar on the sweet consent of holy song ever arising in nature. The lowly valley of Bunyan's Shepherd Boy had as much delight as the Delectable Mountains themselves. Do not be greatly concerned when wrong is done you. Possess your soul in patience. Hide under the wing of God. Do not let anything rob you of your power of being glad with children, birds, flowers, humble and innocent joys.

Without doubt the time is coming when the world itself will be conquered by the meekness and gentleness of Christ and His saints. The gentle dawn will master the blustering night; the soft-treading spring will quell the storms of winter. The knights of the cross, clad in the soft garments of holiness and gentleness, shall yet dissipate the dark squadrons of sin.

Wouldst thou have this meekness? There is no fountain from which it flows save that opened in the heart of Christ, and communicated by the Spirit of God, whose fruit it is. How meekly the Spirit of God has borne with the strife, rejection, contradiction of men. What consummate meekness was ever manifested by our

holy Lord!   Let us abide in Him, asking that
He will repeat in us His characteristic grace,
and enable us to breathe again upon the world
the spirit by which He was animated in life
and death.

O Meek and Gentle Saviour, who, when Thou
wast reviled, reviledst not again, when Thou didst
suffer, threatenedst not, give me of Thy Spirit,
that I may be calm and strong in the endurance
of wrong, and overcome evil with good.

V

HUNGRY—THIRSTY—FILLED

" Blessed are they that hunger and thirst after righteousness: for they shall be filled."—MATT. v. 6.

THIS characteristic of hunger and thirst arises naturally out of the foregoing ones. Up to this we have considered the *passive* side of Christian character—the poverty of spirit that lies low before God, and dares not think of itself more than a redeemed sinner may—the sorrow that mourns in secret over the evil of the world and of the heart—the meekness which has learned to take rebuff, rebuke, and injury calmly and quietly. But now the *active* element begins to assert itself. The man whose face has been buried in the dust, or stained with tears, or covered with marks of contumely and reproach, now lifts it towards God, crying, with David, "As the hart panteth after the water brooks, so panteth my soul after Thee, O God." You misjudged him. You thought that he was altogether deficient in force, and unable to exert himself; now you discover that the whole strength of his nature passes through channels which elude the common view of men, and shows itself in vehement passion towards the Unseen and Eternal.

The desire of the regenerate soul is not simply towards God, but for righteousness. To be right, to do right, to conform in all things to the outlines and spirit of God's ideal, to have a conscience void of offence, to be uncondemned by the heart—this is the desire of the soul. It is not enough to be conscious of weakness and ignorance, or to mourn for sin; the true penitent desires to learn the secret of walking before God in holiness and righteousness all his days.

Our one regret should be that our desires after God and His righteousness are so fickle and faint. There is pain in hunger; nothing is more terrible than to suffer thirst bred by the heat and sand of the desert. But how rarely do we meet with biographies and experiences that come within measurable comparison with these natural cravings for food and drink! Why is it? May we not ask how to increase and augment this hunger for God, so that we shall not need to exert so strong an outward pressure on ourselves to observe times of prayer and worship, but shall leap out in desire towards God and the remembrance of His name, desiring these as the hungry man counts the moments to his meal? Let us take it to heart that we know so little of those passionate yearnings for God which have dwelt in all holy hearts, and the lack of which is one of the most serious signs of declension in the inner life. May God create in us hunger and thirst like that which Jesus knew, even though it should introduce a new and constant pain into our lives, that we may be led by it to know the blessedness that the knowledge and love of God can bring.

I. The Spiritual Appetite.

It results from the constitution of our nature.—We cannot go deeper than nature. We cannot go behind or beyond it, for *nature* is what has been born (Lat. *natura*), born out of God's thought by God's power. When we speak of nature we must pass in thought from her to her parent God, and find a sufficient answer to all questions and difficulties by saying, " God has so willed it, therefore it is as it is."

All the strong basal instincts of human nature must be traced back to the make of our moral being as it was planned by Almighty wisdom, and wrought by infinite power. Do you ask why a belief in the immortality of the soul, and the hereafter, is found in every nation under heaven? Why lying, theft, and murder are accompanied with the blush of shame, and the desire of concealment; why, in the oldest settlements of man, there are traces of the altar and temple: and why human hearts are irresistibly drawn towards each other, finding indissoluble and indestructible affinities? It is only possible to answer by saying, " These things are as they are from the very nature with which God has endowed us." They are necessary, constitutional, essential, as much so as the features of the face, and the general principles of mathematics and arithmetic.

We hunger and thirst, because our physical

nature has been so created that it must needs go out of itself for its supplies of nutriment. No one of one of us is self-contained, or independent of the great world of which we form a part. The difficulties and questions of how it came to be so do not alter the fact. Similarly, God made our souls for Himself. Deep within us, He has put necessities and desires, that crave for satisfaction from the Unseen, Eternal, and Divine.

We have a vision of the land of righteousness and blessedness from which we have come. Trailing clouds of glory, our race has descended into this murky atmosphere, but it can never forget the note of perfect music which it once heard, the vision of perfect beauty which it once beheld. Man is haunted by the thought of God, his original home; and however low he is plunged in sin and wickedness, he does not utterly forget; and there will be a time in his life when the gagged, imprisoned, drugged soul, will arise and come forth and begin to cry with exceeding bitterness, " I have perverted that which was right, and it profited me not " ; " Thy Spirit is good ; lead me into the land of uprightness " ; " I have gone astray like a lost sheep ; seek Thy servant."

5

It produces pain.—There are many sources of pain; but perhaps primarily God has instituted it to compel us to take measures for our health and safety. The intense suffering produced by the decaying tooth is intended to force us to conserve an implement so necessary to mastication. The pain of hunger and thirst is designed to force us to take food, without which the body would become exhausted and die. How tenderly the love of God deals with His children when He forces them by pain to take measures for their own preservation!

So in the moral sphere, we should be thankful, when we are discontented with ourselves, when in self-abhorrence we cry out for God's unsullied righteousness, when we turn from the tortuous policy with loathing, when we go about smitten with infinite unrest. Treasure such an experience, for thus the grace of God leads back to Himself. The "vanity of vanities" of Ecclesiastes, so often wrung from Solomon's soul, was the one symptom of returning health.

It is universal.—As we have never met man or woman incapable of hunger or thirst, so there is no human soul which is not capable of possessing God, and does not need Him for a complete life. Often the spiritual appetite is dormant, as that of a man debauched with drink. The child, whose stomach is cloyed with sweets; the invalid, who has long suffered under the pressure of a wasting illness, may have no appetite, but at any moment it may awake. Thus with the hunger of the soul for God. It awoke in the woman that was a sinner, in the thief on the cross, and Zacchæus the publican. Take it bitterly to heart if it has not gnawed at your complacency, and destroyed your peace. Be very anxious if you know no yearnings for a better life, no desires after righteousness, no dissatisfaction with the present, no tireless search for God. These are grave symptoms.

Reduce all the activities of man to their ultimate reason, and it will be discovered to be as Jesus said—What shall we eat? What shall we drink? Wherewithal shall we be clothed? Perhaps in these northern climes we might add, How shall we be housed? These elemental necessities are the motor forces of the world. Similarly, all the feverish quest of men in music, art, the love of beauty, the pursuit of the chief good, to say nothing of religion, may be traced back to the desire of the soul for something which it has not attained. It

cannot be satisfied in itself. It does not always
know what it needs, any more than the babe does
who feels the pains of hunger, and cries passionately
or bitterly. During the great famines in China and
India, the natives have fed on a kind of edible
earth, making it into loaves. It has stayed their
cravings, but they have grown gradually weaker
till they have lain down to die. The *nardoo* plant
of Australia closely resembles flour, but lacks the
nutritive property, and those who feed on it, though
insensible of hunger, after a few weeks die of
starvation. Thus men who seek for that which is
not bread, who refuse the fair loaf of God's gift,
which is Christ, and feed on ashes, may succeed in
stilling the cravings for the unseen and eternal,
and yet perish of that fatal lack of God.

II. The Nurture of Spiritual Appetite.

We know too little of it. We cannot always say
with the Psalmist, "I was glad when they said
unto me, Let us go into the house of the Lord";
nor yet "My soul breaketh for the longing that it
hath unto Thy judgments at all times"; nor with

Job, "I have esteemed the words of His mouth more than my necessary food."

Here are a few simple directions for the stimulating of our desire for God.

Beware of the other food you take.—When children are unable to take the meal their mother has provided, she suspects them of having visited the confectioner's shop on their way home from school, so that their appetite has become cloyed and sickly. May it not be that before we can have an eager taste for God's Word, we shall have to put away some of the reading in which we now indulge, and which is little better than garbage? Sensational novels, frivolous talk, indulgence in appetite and sense, quickly incapacitate us for enjoying God.

Take exercise.—The more we do, the more food we require, and the more we enjoy it. Manly sports; long, vigorous walks; muscular exertion of any kind, will supply the sauce of hunger which will make the roughest food palatable; and it is they whose hand is seldom off the plough, who sow beside all waters, and are instant in season and out of season, that are most glad when the bells call to rest and food.

Take a tonic.—There is no tonic for spiritual

appetite to compare to the biography of a holy life.
It is well to have such an one constantly at hand.
Frequently the story of the exercises of a man's
soul before God has started others on a more
passionate quest for the Holy Grail.

Get up into the mountains.—The best appetite
invigorator is the keen, bracing air, which breathes
around those natural altars of the world which God
has reared, where the pines grow, and the glacier
moves slowly down, and the sounds of the valley
seem far away. There is nothing so healthy as to
go up with Christ into the high mountain apart
when He prays. The tides of blood are aërated
by the purer atmosphere ; the eye sparkles with
clearer vision ; the appetite of the soul becomes
keener.

Let us never rest with low levels, attenuated
aspirations, or the mean standards which content
our fellows. The only hope of the young artist
is that he should not be content with the standard
that prevails in the provincial town of his birth,
but aim after that presented in the highest master-
pieces. The only hope of the cygnet, born in the
farmyard, is that it should not be content to paddle
in the pond which suffices for the ducks. The

hope of the soul is to refuse comparison with those beneath, and to keep the eye fixed on the righteousness of God as it is revealed in the life and words of Jesus. "Not as though I had already attained, but I press on." Let us see to it that we apply the highest standards of right to ourselves, to our relations with our fellow-men, and to our attitude before God, so that we could be content to live alone with God, as the one all-satisfying food of the soul. Hudson Taylor said the other day, " I have been forty years in China, it is forty years since I first landed on her shores, I have *done* but little there, I have *learnt* much, and this of all things —to live alone with God, to know God Himself, to know that His heart is love, and that His heart actuates His hand to help." Here is an ideal after which we may well aspire.

III. THE CERTAIN GRATIFICATION OF THIS APPETITE.

God never sends mouths, the old proverb says, but He sends with them the food to fill them. Young lions never seek that which His hand does not open to give. The fish, and the fly at which

it snatches; the bird, and the berries on the
hawthorn bush; the babe, and the milk stored
in its mother's breast, are perfectly adapted to
each other. The instinct for immortality, and the
mansions which Christ has gone to prepare; the
desire for the city, and the city which hath foundations; the lively hope to which we are begotten
by the resurrection of Christ, and its fruition, are
in perfect harmony. Whatever you and I have
longed for in our best and holiest moments, may
have its consummation and bliss, because God
has prepared for our perfect satisfaction. No
hunger without food to match it; no wing without air to match it; no fire without water to
match it; no babe's cry without the mother's
love to match it; and no soul hungering and
thirsting after the righteousness of God without
God to meet and match it.

Do you ask what is the bread of God, which
can satisfy the insatiable craving of man's heart?
Jesus says, "I am that Bread of Life, he that
cometh to Me shall never hunger; he that
believeth in Me shall never thirst. I am the
Bread of Life which came down from heaven,
of which a man may eat and not die. The

Bread that I shall give is my Flesh that I shall
give for the life of the world. He that drinketh
of the water that I shall give shall never thirst."

Christ is made unto us righteousness. In other
words, the man who has Christ, and gets right
with Him, who is brought into adjusted relation-
ship with Christ, almost unconsciously gets right
with himself, with men, with the great system of
law, and with God. Do not fret about the infinite
demands that surround you. Do one thing. Let
Christ be Alpha and Omega. With Him as
foundation-stone, your building shall stand four-
square to God and man.

Are you filled? Do you know what it is to be
satisfied? Have you ever been filled? Has it
ever occurred to you to ask what the apostle
meant by saying that the disciples were complete
in Him? If not, and you truly desire these
experiences, God will supply all your need out
of His riches in glory. To ask, is to have. To
seek, is to receive. To hunger and thirst, is to
be satisfied. Lift up your heart unto the Lord,
and say, " Fill me." Cry for Him with an
exceeding great cry. For bread He will not
give a stone or a serpent for fish. Believe that

you receive simultaneously with your request, and you will know the blessedness of the pain which has brought you to God, the blessedness of being satisfied from God, the blessedness of desiring more of God ; and yours shall be the song of the Virgin Mother — "He hath filled the hungry with good things." "My soul shall be satisfied as with marrow and fatness; and my mouth shall praise Thee with joyful lips."

To Thee, O Lord, I come with desires which Thou hast implanted, and alone canst satisfy; give me Thyself; for Thee I was made, and apart from Thee I cannot find rest or satisfaction. Thy flesh is meat indeed, and Thy blood drink indeed.

VI

IT GOETH FORTH AND RETURNETH

" Blessed are the merciful : for they shall obtain mercy."
—MATT. v. 7.

NOTICE where our Saviour puts this beatitude, the heart of which is mercy. It follows that longing after righteousness which is the characteristic of the righteous, because mercy is the white flower on the stem of a righteous life. Indeed, the absence of mercy in our temper and disposition shows that our righteousness is that of the ceremonialist, as that of Saul, who was blameless as touching the righteousness which is of the law, but utterly devoid of those Christian virtues which indicate the presence of the truly holy heart. The religion which is devoid of mercy is that of the exterior form, but destitute of the inward power. It was therefore with a Divine insight that our Lord put mercy after righteousness—first, because a man must be right before he can be merciful; and second, he must be rightly adjusted with the Fountain of mercy so that the Divine quality of mercy can pass unhindered through him, and approve him to be a son of the All - Merciful. Search your heart, and see if you have learnt forgiveness for the sinning, and pity for the sorrowful; not otherwise can you account yourself righteous after God's fashion.

Mercy is the exclusive prerogative of Christianity. The schools of ancient morality had four cardinal virtues — justice in human relations, prudence in the direction of affairs, fortitude in bearing trouble and sorrow, temperance or self-restraint; but they knew nothing of mercy, which is not natural to the human heart. It is an exotic which Christ brought with Him from heaven. As long as the Lord Jesus tarried amongst men, He poured forth mercy in its double form of forgiveness and succour, to those that hated and to those that were wronged; and when He passed back to the Father, the Church took up His blessed work, and came to the world, as the dew distilling on the parched pastures, to become the saviour and regenerator of society. She found the most horrible practices in vogue, which she stayed; the most preposterous customs, which she tempered; amusements and games, which she discountenanced and finally abolished. She extended her beneficent sceptre to captives, and women oppressed with innumerable wrongs, and little children. Regardless of her own sufferings, she existed apparently for the sole reason of ministering to those that wronged and oppressed her, as well as to those who were being trampled under foot by greed and lust and hate. Thus mercy sprang out of the ground in response to the righteousness which looked down from heaven.

I. THE QUALITY OF MERCY.

It is evidently a phase of love, for each of these beatitudes enshrines some aspect of the Love of God in the soul of man.

The first is Love in her humility, with such

great thoughts of the possibilities within her reach that she counts herself not to have attained.

The second is Love in tears, bewailing the lovelessness of the world.

The third is Love suffering wrong in the hope of vanquishing it.

The fourth is Love impelled by insatiable desire for fuller satisfaction.

The fifth, of which we are now treating, is Love retaliating on wrong.

The sixth is Love burning with a faith so pure that evil cannot withstand.

The seventh is Love so equable that it can quiet and steady anger and strife.

The eighth is Love misunderstood and persecuted.

Each is therefore a facet on which the sunlight falls, and from which it is reflected at a new angle, and with a new beauty. Let the love of God dwell in you richly, and as it passes out from you to strike the many evils of the world, each phase of sin will elicit and reflect some special quality. Some day it may appear that sin was permitted, in order to set forth the perfect beauty of Divine love, just as clouds unravel the contents of the light into rainbow hues.

There is a distinction between Meekness and Merci-fulness.—Meekness is the passive, mercy the active side of Love. The meek man entering into union with the love of God, which is ever-suffering beneath the wrong of the world, and knowing that the power of evil will presently be broken by meek forbearance, suffers with the long-suffering of God. But mercy goes further. It takes measures with the wrong-doer. In mercy our love issues forth towards the perpetrator of injury, pitying, bending down with tender hand and gentle touch, pouring in oil and wine, and endeavouring, by the coals of fire it heaps on the offender, to melt his obdurate heart, and bring him to a happier state. Mercy seeks out the wrong-doer, if so be that it may lead him to repentance, notices the first symptom of return and meets it, welcomes him with kisses, undoes the injury which he has wrought to himself, and reinstates him in the old place.

There is also some difference between mercy and forgiveness. Love is the parent and root of all. Grace is love coming forth to meet those who had forfeited all claim upon it. Forgiveness is love assuring the wrong-doer that the past is forgotten. Mercy tries to ameliorate the condition of the sinner. Whenever wrong is done you, think less of what you suffer than of the state of his heart, its darkness and misery, who has done the ill, and when you have conceived of it, seek to alleviate it. This is mercy.

II. The Circumstances which awake Mercy.

First, Sin.—In Psalm li. we have the plaintive cry of a broken heart. " Have mercy upon me, O God, according to Thy lovingkindness : according unto the multitude of Thy tender mercies blot out my transgressions . . . against Thee, Thee only, have I sinned . . . that the bones which Thou hast broken may rejoice." Forgiveness is not enough, the broken bones cry out for mending. Forgiveness does not necessarily include reparation of the hurt, which wrong-doing inflicts on the wrong-doer. The drunkard may be forgiven, and yet have to bear the results of injury to his body and nerve ; nevertheless, when such an one is forgiven, he may also count on the mercy of God, pitying that trembling, palsied hand, and that wrecked constitution, and endeavouring so far as may be possible, to undo the havoc, and to bring again his flesh as fair as that of a little child. Thus mercy rejoices against judgment.

Second, Suffering.—Luke x. 37 tells of the mercy of the stranger to which even the Scribe bore unwilling testimony. "Which of these," asked the Lord, after He had vividly portrayed Priest, Levite, and Samaritan, "proved neighbour to him that fell among the thieves?" And the Scribe was compelled to admit, "He that showed mercy on him."

In such a state of things as that which surrounds us in any great city, we must be careful to allow our mercy to flow freely forth. Nothing is worse than to be always checking it from fear of imposition. Better to be deceived and wronged now and again, than to be always withholding the hand. We must take care, of course, not to harm men by encouraging them in idleness and lying fraud. It is the truest mercy often to withhold the dole of charity from those who would misspend it. We must see to it, also, that we are not content with the impulsive act of benevolence, which flings some coin to the outstretched hand to save itself the

6

trouble of investigating the need, and ascertaining the best way of meeting it. Mercy may refuse to give on the spur of the moment, that it may help permanently and efficiently. We must be very careful, also, not to entrust the giving of our alms to the paid hand of agents and professional almoners. Organised charity is a symptom of a Christianity which retains the name of Christ, but from which His Spirit has fled. If mercy is to rise spontaneously and perennially, it must be nurtured by personal contact with sorrow and suffering. Its own hands must bind the sores, and smooth the pillow, and arrange the disordered room, and watch through the night-vigils.

Third, Ignorance and Infirmities.—Hebrews ii. 17, x. 15. Our Lord Jesus is a merciful and faithful High Priest . . . touched with the feeling of our infirmities, and able to have compassion on the ignorant and erring.

Mercy does not wait for sorrow and need to appeal to her. She goes to seek them. She does not wait for the injury to be wrought on her, before being prompted to retaliate in heaven's own kind, but her lovely form casts a light as it passes through the squalid street, climbing the creaking staircase, and pursuing the victims of the great wrong of the world where they hide their festering sores. Oh, beautiful is the light on Mercy's face, when she beholds some scene of want and woe, from which the refinement and culture of the world would turn, disgusted and loathing. This is work that she loves. Here she is in her element. She needs no teaching, for the heaven-born instincts of her heart prompt her. Her voice is musical with the tones of the Incarnate Saviour. Her hand is deft and soft. Her tread is beautiful as it passes along the mountain track, rugged, storm-swept, difficult to the foot. To have seen her would make you think that you had met one of the daughters of the family of God.

III. THE BENEDICTION.

It has been noticed that the three first beatitudes touch the lower plane of our experience by which need has to be met with its opposite. Hence the blessedness consists in imparting the appropriate satisfaction, but the fifth, sixth, and seventh—that is, the three which lie on the hither side of desire —are those of the saint, whose blessedness consists

in having more of the quality already possessed.
Hence, mercy is the appropriate reward of those
who already show it.

Have you ever noticed the way in which *these
attributes of the blessed life demand the coming of
the Comforter.* Matthew v. demands John xv.
and xvi. The commandments of the forty days
demand the gift of Pentecost. The traits of
Christian character must be burnt in by the
Baptism of Fire. There must be a power yet
to be revealed by which these rare and precious
exotics may be made to bloom on the wintry soil
of the soul. The law of love is given in all its
fulness on this mount of beatitudes, as the law of
righteousness amid the thunders of Sinai, that being
hopeless of ourselves, we may be shut up to faith
in the Holy Ghost, who alone can work in us the
fruit of the Divine life. "The fruit of the Spirit
is love, joy, peace, long-suffering, gentleness,
meekness . . . ."

*The merciful alone experience all the mercifulness of
God.*—It was after Job had pitied and prayed for
his friends that his own captivity was brought
again. "See," says the apostle, "the end of the
Lord, that He is full of pity, and merciful." If we

go through the world ministering to others, God
will come and minister to us. His angels will
come around us with their gentle ministry, doing
for us as we have sought to do for others.
"Blessed is he that considereth the poor, the Lord
will remember him in time of trouble."

In one of His most striking parables our Lord
depicts the forgiven steward, who took his brother
by the throat, demanding payment, as forfeiting
the clemency which his lord's mercy had brought
him. "Shouldest not thou also have had mercy
on thy fellow-servant, as I had mercy upon thee?
And he delivered him up to the tormentors."
That cannot mean that God ever withdraws His
mercy from the soul He has once forgiven, because
God cannot change His mind, but it means surely
that the unmerciful cannot claim God's mercy.
If, therefore, thou hast not forgiven, thou hast
not been forgiven. Each time you utter the
Lord's Prayer—Forgive, according to the measure
of my own forgiveness—you really say, Do not
forgive me because I have not forgiven, and I
dare not ask Thee to do for me what I have
not done to my brother sinner.

Be sure that in coming days you will need

forgiveness, more, perhaps, than you realise, for you do not know yourself; but, at such a time, the failure to show mercy will arise, and, lifting its voice, will plead against you and overpower your plea for forgiveness.

The merciful may count on mercy from their fellows. —None are treated so mercilessly as the merciless. With what measure ye mete it shall be measured to you again. Let anyone be censorious in criticism, vindictive and malicious, quick to resent a wrong, bitter and uncharitable in speech, relentless in demanding reparation; and the time will come when that soul will need mercy from its fellows, and meet the stolid stare of indifference. " And Adonibezek said, Threescore and ten kings, having their thumbs and their great toes cut off, gathered their meat under my table: as I have done, so God hath requited me."

On the other hand, those who are tender and gentle in their judgment, patient and forbearing in disposition, peaceable and easy to be entreated, quick to forgive the wrong-doer, and to repair the wrong, will never be in need of mercy, but in hours of darkness and peril, forgotten acts of kindness will arise from long-buried seeds, and mercy which had gone forth to bless others will return from its long journey and many errands, in time to comfort and requite the heart from which it started forth. "Blessed are the merciful, for they shall obtain mercy."

How great has been Thy goodness to me, O Lord, who am not worthy of the least of all Thy mercies; make me tender and forgiving to my fellow-servants, as Thou hast been to me; that their hearts may, in turn, be softened, and taught the law of mercy and long-suffering.

VII

THE BEATIFIC VISION

" Blessed are the pure in heart: for they shall see God."
—MATT. v. 8.

OF all the eight beatitudes, none arrests us
with a greater sense of sublimity and
majesty than this; and none, in its possession,
more absolutely distinguishes the religion of the
Lord Jesus Christ. Like some inaccessible Alpine
peak, covered with virgin snow, this conception of
the pure heart towers up amid all the great words
of this marvellous discourse.

To be pure in behaviour and life was admitted
by the Stoics to be the sign and token of true
manhood; but to be pure in heart has been
deemed an inaccessible and untenable position.

Even if it were Christ's by the peculiar constitution of His nature, it cannot, so men argue, become the attribute of natures which were conceived in sin and shapen in iniquity, and are impressed with the evil impulses of generations of self-indulgence. To know sin only to abhor it, to keep so strong a hold on appetite that, like some spirited horse, it shall only fulfil its legitimate purpose, to be always blameless and harmless, to wear ever the white flower of a stainless life, to allow no lewd visitant to cross the threshold of the soul, to permit no foul picture to remain for a moment on the lens of the inner eye, to love all men and women with a pure and unselfish affection in which there is no taint or stain—this is an ideal which, if it flitted before the minds of men like a bright vision, was not attained until Jesus came with that omnific word, which said to the leper, " I will, be thou clean," and in that early miracle gave a sign of the characteristic of His life, in saving those who had been deeply dyed in the ditch of sensual indulgence, and making them bright jewels in His crown. Thus pure white paper is woven from rags, and diamonds manufactured out of charcoal.

PURITY OF HEART WILL ENSURE PURITY OF LIFE AND CONDUCT.

This connection has been too often overlooked, and the order forgotten. Many have insisted on the careful regimen of the body, frugal diet, vigorous exercise, cleanliness of person; and have reiterated the ancient maxims of the Stoical philosophy—Touch not, Taste not, Handle not; though discovering, as the apostle said, long ago, that these things have indeed a show of will-worship, and humility, and severity to the body, but are not of any value against the indulgence of the flesh.

No, the secret of purity lies deeper. Begin with the outward, and you may or may not affect the inward temper of the soul. Begin with the inward temper, and the effect on the outward will be immediate and transfiguring.

Purity of heart means *the control of the imagination*. Away from the realm of sense there lies a world of illusion, the atmosphere of which is brilliant but deadly, its scenery bewitching but corrupting, the inhabitants wicked spirits, some of whom are robed in exquisite costumes veiling their deformity, whilst others are at no pains to hide their loathsomeness. Thither imagination can at will transport us. Like a swift shallop it can convey us to those mystic shores ; and disembarking we can take our part in unseemly revels, whilst our face is buried in our hands, in the attitude of prayer, or our outward presence is sharing in the amenities of the home-circle. But no heart can be kept pure, unless the fancy is kept sternly under control. It must not be permitted to bear us away into the world of unholy and sensuous dreams, or to introduce into the temple of the soul any picture which would taint or defile.

Purity of heart means *the rigorous care of the affections*. We must love. Not to love is to lose God and heaven out of life ; not to love is to miss the inner secret of blessedness ; not to love is to deny the exercise of our noblest powers. We wrong the nature with which God has endowed us when we refuse to love. But our affections resemble the tendrils of clinging plants, they reach out altogether in wrong directions, or too profusely in right ones. So our love strays to those to whom we ought not to give it, or overflows with undue extravagance to those who have a claim to something but not all. Nothing is more hurtful than a friendship which monopolises all the thought and force of the lovers, to the exclusion of all others, and especially of God. We must love God in others, and them in God, only where His will permits, and to the extent which is compatible with His claims for the first place. Whenever you feel your heart giving out strongly to another, be very careful to consider whither the strong tide is bearing you, and stay whilst yet it is possible to resist its current.

The intention of the soul must be single.—To do God's will, whatever it costs; to follow in the line of His command, whatever it involves; to live within the limits He has laid down, whatever be the solicitation to outstep them. The eye must be single. The soul must resolve within itself that it will absolutely yield to God, though the surrender involve the loss of all beside. Impurity, when traced to its source, will often be found to arise from a lack of decision that God's way and will shall be paramount, and that nothing shall be permitted, even for a moment, to conflict with them.

The attitude of the will is also all-important.—
This, after all, is the key to the position. The
will is the custodian of the soul. Conscience
pleads as the prophet and priest of God; the
affection and emotions put in their passionate
plea; memory recites the results of past experience; the imagination presents vivid portrayals
of the consequences of certain acts; the judgment
sits upon the bench, sums up and gives its
decision; but, after all, it is for the will to act.
We may almost say that it holds the destinies of
life, at its belt swings the key with which it opens
and none shuts, with which it shuts and none
opens. The will is like the front wheel of the
bicycle, which gives the direction to the movements
of the machine; it resembles the steersman of
the packet, standing weather-beaten behind the
wheel; it is the prime minister of the inner
court, its executive and marshal.

Oh, that thou and I, my reader, may choose
purity above all, setting our will towards it with
understanding tenacity, preferring it above our
chief good, ever prepared to surrender everything
if only this may be our lot, to count no sacrifice
too great, no cliff too steep! Dost thou not think

that God would meet us, and accomplish that on
which our decisions were fixed? Could He lead
us to such high resolves, only to disappoint and
mock? Is not the conception of such a state a
prophecy of what God is prepared to realise?
Surely it is not in vain that His Spirit has indited
the prayer, "Cleanse Thou the thoughts of our
hearts by the inspiration of Thy Holy Spirit, that
we may perfectly serve Thee, and worthily magnify
Thy holy name."

The Law of Purity is Clearly Revealed.

It is the great gift of the gospel to teach men
that Purity is possible — possible for those who
have suffered most from the law of a depraved
heredity, possible to those whose habits of evil
living and thinking have been most debased,
possible for those who have striven in vain to
keep the marble palace of the inner life from
being defiled by the tides of ink which sweep
through the world. Let anyone follow the
Divine prescription, they will find the vision of
the pure in heart is not a dream, but that the

Lord Jesus is prepared to do for the inner life
what He did for the leprous flesh. He can effect
in our experience that temper of soul which knows
evil only to abhor it, which is conscious of the
presence of the tempter only to loathe his suggestion, which detects the hideous form beneath
the dazzling garb of one who appears to be an
angel of light. Remember the words of the
apostle in which he reminded his converts that
they had been delivered from the powers of
darkness, and been translated into the kingdom
of light and love, the kingdom of God's dear
Son.

And what is the prime condition of this heart-
purity? The answer comes back clear and sufficient from the lips of Peter, when speaking of
God's work through him amongst the Gentiles.
"God," says he, "which knoweth the heart, bear
them witness, giving them the Holy Ghost, and
He made no distinction between us and them,
cleansing their hearts by faith."

And how does Faith cleanse the heart? There
are many ways in which she performs her holy
office.

She brings the soul to the Cross, and bids it

behold the dying Saviour, and asks how, in view
of such sorrow and anguish, borne to put away
its sin, it can ever dare to open those wounds
again, or add one stab of pain to that infinite
agony.

She applies to the soul the precious blood of
Christ that cleanseth from all sin, and there is
nothing which so effectively produces inward
purity as forgiveness based upon the sacrifice of
the Redeemer. The ease with which the penitent
and believing heart can claim forgiveness does not
conduce to sin, but begets a holy fear which makes
it increasingly abhorrent.

She has the marvellous power of handing over
to Christ every suggestion of the Evil One.
Whilst the fiery dart is flaming through the air,
and before it reaches the soul, Faith catches it
upon her shield. When the sooty hand is reached
out to pluck her white flower, Faith suddenly in-
terposes the protective covering of the purity of
Christ. To hand over to Jesus every approaching
temptation, each evil suggestion, all haunting
fancies, when as yet they are in the air, and have
not put their foot within the threshold of the soul,
is the lesson which faith teaches.

But better than all, Faith appropriates the Purity of Christ. In the moment of temptation she lifts her thought and prayer to Him to claim that His purity should so fill the soul with its perfect heat and light, that there should be no room for impurity to lurk in any corner. Perhaps it would be better to say that Faith appropriates Christ as its purity, rather than the Purity of Christ. A person must always help us better than an attribute, and Christ Himself is made more to us than any single quality of His nature. The whole is greater than its part.

It has been discovered that there is no bacillus that can withstand sunlight, and certainly no impurity can remain in the heart which is perfectly filled with the presence of Christ, maintained there by the grace of the Holy Ghost. Darkness cannot coexist with light. Let the light in, and the darkness needs no other method of expurgation. It seems to me needless to stay to argue whether the root of sin is extracted or not; the one point is to let the refiner of silver pass our nature through the baptism of fire of which the Baptist spoke, when he foretold that the Lamb of God should baptize with the Holy Ghost, and with fire. When once the refining fire has passed through the heart, and is maintained within it, purity will be as natural as breathing to a man, as singing to a happy child.

The Guerdon is Transcendently Attractive.

"*They shall see God.*"—To see the king's face was the object of ambition to loyal courtiers and subjects in the old days, when the Queen of Sheba congratulated the servants of Solomon on being able to stand always before him. And to Absalom it was the keenest sign of disgrace that he was not allowed to see the face of the king, his father.

This is the thought that probably underlies this beatitude. Only the pure in heart can stand in the inner circle, searched by those eyes that are too pure to look upon sin. Only garments which are unstained can pass muster in the throne-room of the Supreme. This truth was symbolised in the purity of ablution, ceremonial and dress, which prevailed in the ancient tabernacle; and it remains true for ever that without holiness no man can see the Lord. If, then, you and I would dwell in the secret place of the Most High, and abide under the shadow of the Almighty; if we would dwell in the house of the Lord all the days of our life, we must be pure in heart.

The pure in heart see. They are seers. They get at truth first-hand. They see God in nature, beneath each flower, and tree, and waterfall; they see Him in every incident of providence; and circumstance does but reveal His plan and is as the slight gauze that conceals His movements; they see Him in human love, and tender voices, in the caress of the little child, and faithfulness of the true woman; they see Him in Scripture which burns like the bush of the desert because He is there; and their most cherished aspiration is to behold His face in righteousness, and to be satisfied when they awake with His likeness.

It is good to have the eye of the soul cleansed, that it may see what prophets and kings have been unable to discover by the exercise of the intellect. It is of this spiritual lens that the apostle speaks when he says, He that is spiritual discerneth all things, though he is himself discerned by no man. Even here and now we see God, but what will not

be our rapture when this gross veil of flesh and
infirmity is rent in twain from the top to the
bottom, and we are permitted to stand before
the throne, because the garments of the soul have
been washed and made white in the blood of the
Lamb!

In Thee was no sin, my Saviour; Thou wast
the guileless, spotless Lamb of God; baptize me
into the Fire of Thy Purity, and let me walk
with Thee in pure unspotted robes.

VIII

SWORDS INTO PRUNING-HOOKS

" Blessed are the peacemakers: for they shall be called the sons of God."—MATT. v. 9.

THE utterance of this beatitude indicates the state of the world, as indeed all the beatitudes do. From these photographs of the characteristics of the children of God we may learn the characteristics of the world out of which they have come. We know that we are of God, because we have learnt something of this poverty of spirit, this Divine sorrow, this meekness, this hunger, this mercy, this purity; but we know, also, that the whole world around us is as the direct antipodes of these holy qualities. We are learning to be poor in spirit, but the world is proud; we mourn, with

bitter tears, over our own sin and the sins of the
world, but the world sins without tears. We know
what it is in some small measure to bear insult
patiently, but the world proudly resents insult.
We are conscious of a Divine hunger and thirst
after the eternal righteousness, without which the
unrest of our heart will never be content, whilst
the men around us are satisfied if their senses and
appetites are satisfied. We know something of
what it is to have the love of God pouring through
us in merciful kindness towards the evil that would
work us injury, whilst the world knows no mercy,
but men take their brothers by the throat, saying,
"Pay me what thou owest." We know a little of
that yearning for the snow-clad peaks of purity,
whilst we recognise that the world lies in the power
of the Evil One, and we have only just escaped
the corruption which is in the world through lust.

The strong emphasis which our Saviour lays on
peacemaking shows the world around to be full of
peacebreaking, and so devoid of God's halcyon rest.
Is it not because men have lost the Fatherhood
that they have lost the Brotherhood? The tender
love of the father to the child, and the father's
love recognised by the child, is the great bond and

tie of the home-circle, widened to include the universe. But since men have lost the consciousness of the love of God, and have lost, in consequence, the responsive love which should go forth to Him from their heart, they are consumed by the greed, lust, jealousy, hatred, and suspicion which are at the root of the peacelessness of the world. Therefore God calls us, His little children, to His side, in Jesus Christ, and He says, "Children, I have a great work on hand in the world; all the universe beside is in peace except your little planet and its surrounding atmosphere, in which the devil and his angels have their seat; but I can never rest until My peace has overcome the strife and war and discord of the human family and of the devil realm that prompts it: come, therefore, and I will send you forth, and your feet shall be beautiful upon the mountains as you publish peace. My sons and daughters, help Me to bring peace again to man; be peacemakers, and so inherit the blessedness of God."

Now we will notice, first, the qualifications which are necessary to the peacemaker; secondly, the method in which he shall do his work; thirdly, the abundant recognition which it will secure.

I. The Qualifications of the Peacemaker.

This beatitude follows the one in which our Saviour shows the bliss of the pure heart: "Blessed are the pure in heart, for they shall see God."

The order of these beatitudes is extremely instructive, and one leads to the other like the steps of a great staircase ever upward to the climax. Obviously *purity of heart must precede peacemaking*; and for this reason — that it is only the pure of heart who can see God, and it is only in so far as we see God going forth to make peace that we can follow His example. As it was true of Christ, so it is true of us, all true living must be the reflection of what we see the Father doing (John v. 19). This is a very profound thought, and it certainly underlay the entire ministry of our blessed Saviour, so that everything He did was the reflection of the movements of His Father's nature. When He wrought in the creation of the universe He was working out the creative thought of His Father; and when He stepped out from His Throne and the angel's anthem told of " peace on earth, and goodwill towards men," it was only that He might achieve upon our sin-stricken world the deep yearning of the Father's heart for the pacification of its children. When, finally, our Lord Jesus Christ died upon the Cross it was not the act and deed of His loving heart, apart from the Father, but just the repetition and reflection, in terms that man could read and understand, of yearnings and pity in the Father's heart, of which they were the translation. And so all through this wonderful era in which Jesus Christ is still working amongst men to achieve the Divine purposes.

Amongst the many arguments, then, by which we may endeavour to stir ourselves and induce others to become peacemakers, probably the loftiest is the one which leads the Christian constantly to inquire, "What is my Father doing; what is my Father caring for; in which direction are the energies of the Eternal Nature now proceeding, for if I can only discover these, the truest policy for myself, for my blessedness, and the blessedness of others is that I should concur with and advance, so far as I can, those mighty movements." Therefore the purity of heart in which a man sees God seems necessary, as the prerequisite for the peacemaking which is occupying our thoughts. And if, day by

day, before we started forth on our daily pilgrimage,
we were only pure enough in heart to stand before
the presence of the King and to ascertain in which
direction He was most strenuously occupied; to
learn from Him what great design He had in hand;
then, as sons of the Father, and as brothers of
Christ, we should become interested in that in
which He was interested, and enthusiastic over
that upon which He had set His heart. We
should go forth day by day, saying, "Whither are
Thy steps leading, O Prince of Peace? We, Thy
young brothers and sisters, would fain place our
footprints where Thine have left their impress.
There are homes that Thou art entering to allay
fear, unrest and disquietude, we will follow; where
there are hearts that are tossed like the restless
sea, over which Thou art about to speak Thy
'peace be still,' we will breathe it also; and where
healing, rest-giving ministries have to be per-
formed to men, then we will be there, too, to
further Thee in Thy work."

There is not much hope of any of us, with our
limited resources and powers, accomplishing much
of this great work of peacemaking in the world if
we look only to ourselves. But our power is

immensely multiplied when we have learnt to see God; to live in communion with Christ; to open our being to the blessed Holy Spirit, the Dove of Peace, that we may co-operate with God, and, watching Him, may do in earth what He is doing in heaven. "Blessed are the pure in heart: for they shall see God." "Blessed are the peacemakers: for they shall be called sons of God." See how the two are associated.

Secondly, *we must be prepared for sacrifices.* God made peace by blood. It is a very wonderful conception of redemption, which is presented to us in the New Testament. As Shakespeare says, "God who might have vantage took, found out the remedy." It is so wonderful to think that when all our world and race were at war with God—He, so far as He could, and at infinite cost, put out of the way the cause of hostility. But He could only do it at the cost of blood. I confess that I have no plumb-line to fathom all that is meant by making peace through the blood of the Cross. We know that the blood is the life; and that, when on Calvary, the blood of God's Lamb was shed, it was as though the life of the Son of God were poured out. He was the substitute and sacrifice for sin,

though probably there was something deeper even
than this in the draining out of the energy of the
flesh, that being utterly exhausted, helpless as to
His natural life, He might be lifted up to become
the Second Adam, and to give life to men.   These
are deep conceptions.   There is an objective side
in which the death of Christ deals with God's
broken law, and a subjective side in which the
death of Christ somehow deals with our flesh life ;
but all we need to emphasise now is the fact that
when God made peace it was based on righteousness, and the demands of righteousness were met
at the cost of infinite suffering, of which the emblem
is shed blood.   Melchizedek was first the king of
righteousness before he could be the priest of peace.
If righteousness means meeting the claims of a
broken law, which had been violated, and which
man could not meet, then the cost of laying the
deep foundation of righteousness on which the
temple of peace was to be reared, could only be at
infinite cost, the cost of blood ; and if *we* are to
make peace with men it will have to be at heavy cost
to ourselves.   If there is strife between ourselves
and others, as we were once at war with God, it
may be needful for us, at a great cost of tears and

anguish, to remove from between them and us the obstacles to peace. It will cost us something to make and maintain peace. We shall have to sacrifice our pride, reputation, the maintenance of our fancied rights, to say nothing of ease and self-indulgence, if we shall repair the wrong of the evil-doer, and readjust broken relationships. The ambassadors of peace throughout the world have had to expend their very life blood in their endeavour to make peace, consistently with the demands of righteousness. For the most part they have met those demands, that on this basis they might build the temple.

Thirdly, *we should ever carry within us the peace of God.* God is the centre of peace "the God of peace," from whose nature the undulations of ever-widening circlets of peace are spreading through the world. We were once at enmity, but we have been graciously attracted back to Him, and as His children have become filled with His peace. "Let the peace of God rule in your heart." We shall never be able to make peace in the world until we have learnt the secret of peace ourselves. Let Jesus Christ utter His word "Peace be unto you." Let Him show you His hands and His side. Let

Him breathe upon you the spirit of peace, and say,
"Receive the Holy Ghost." Let that peace stand
sentinel at your heart's gate. Be careful to watch
against the intrusion of anxiety, care, and worry,
and whenever these things come, treat them as
Nehemiah did the Tyrian fishwomen, whom he
kept outside the gates of Jerusalem because it was
the Sabbath. Do not let the cries of the world's
fever and tumult break the Sabbath-keeping of
your heart. Live in peace. Rather suffer wrong
than allow peace to be broken on your account.
Follow peace with all men. Carry always in your
heart the serene calm and on your face the placid
look. Let there be no jarring irritated note in
your voice. Let all your movements be consistent
with the rhythm of God's perfect peace. Go
through the world with soft tread, carrying everywhere the atmosphere of God's home. And then
at night, having done all, by your act, your look,
your word, your behaviour, to instil peace into this
troubled world, return back to your Father's bosom,
as a little child who has been at school all day amid
rough companions, but joyfully returns to his home
at night. So go back to the God of peace and
steep your weary soul in His infinite restfulness,

and tell Him all your anxiety for yourself and others. Lean your head back upon His bosom and rest there, and the God of peace will give you peace, and enable you to go forth again on the morrow upon a similiar mission. So we shall shed the peace of heaven over the sorrows and troubles of earth.

II. THE METHOD IN WHICH HE SHALL DO HIS WORK.

There are three or four avenues in which we are to perform this blessed office.

First, *with regard to our own adversaries*—to those who are hostile to us and seeking to harm us. Never lose your peace with such, but see if there is anything you can do, consistently with the claims of honour and justice, even though at heavy cost to yourself, to remove the cause of trouble. Take out of the way, so far as you can, the obstacles to peace. It is better to suffer wrong than to allow some thorn of misunderstanding and ill-will to rankle between yourself and another. St. Paul was very clear against believer going to law with believer; he insisted that it was far better to suffer wrong. And as to our relations with others, it is probably better, after due remonstrance, to suffer than to avenge ourselves. The only thing which really justifies us breaking the outward reign of peace by physical force or by appeal to law is when some evil-doer is carrying out a policy of tyranny, oppression, and high-handed wrong against the defenceless and helpless. In other cases, when there is a cause of misunderstanding, seek out thine adversary, tell him his fault between thee and him alone, try to put away the cause of stumbling and offence, and if worse becomes worst, suffer.

Secondly, *we have to go forth incessantly pouring oil upon the troubled waters.* Not stirring up strife, not suggesting suspicion, but allaying discord, and putting loving and charitable constructions upon things which irritate and annoy. Very often the peacemaker, by a suggestion he makes, by the new light he casts upon a word or action, will allay the irritable feeling which was leading to a breach of peace. We may often mediate between two parties at strife, when our heart is perfectly pure and our eye single and our judgment well balanced.

Thirdly, *we must endeavour to spread counsels of*

peace. Judged by human standards of computation, the progress of peace among men is terribly slow.

It is more than eighteen hundred years now since the angels sang their carol, and yet peace seems still to have fled the world. See the nations of Europe armed to their teeth. Take the daily paper any morning, and glance down the telegrams. Recall the incessant struggle in Parliament and the Law Courts, on the Stock Exchange, in the money markets, and in business. Look into the churches which profess the name of Jesus, and consider the discord and jealousy everywhere. There is plenty of work for the sons of peace to do everywhere, and often their hearts fail and are discouraged. Judged by our standards the dawn is so long in breaking. Men's swords flash so defiantly and suddenly in the air, while counsels of peace are slow as the flower of the cactus-plant. But the morning will break. Meanwhile, every new convert to the great cause of international arbitration, every quarrel that is composed, every passion that is calmed, every sword which is transformed to a pruning-hook, is another step in the great cause which we espoused, when we first ranged ourselves on the side of Christ.

8

Fourthly, *we must urge men to be reconciled to God.*
It is only when the heart is right with God that it
is right universally.   To be wrong with Him, is to
be at war with all beside.   The ill works out.
Diseased blood means boils, and blains, and sores.
The unrestful heart is the source of disturbance
everywhere.   Our one message to man is : God is
at peace with you, be at peace with Him.   He is
reconciled, be ye reconciled.   Sonship will involve
brotherhood.

No such effort is ever lost, no such word ever
falls to the ground, no endeavour to make peace
leaves the peacemaker poorer.   You either have
the satisfaction of seeing your work accomplished,
or the peace of God comes back like the dove to
Noah's ark—" your peace shall return to you."

III. Our Reward.

"You shall be called sons of God."   The
emphasis is on the word *called*.   We are sons to
start with—we could not enter into the Father's
plans if we were not ; but we shall be *called* sons
of God.   As it is said of Christ, that He was

proved to be the Son of God with power by His resurrection—He had been the Son of God before, but He was declared to be so on that day. So, as we go about amongst men, carrying peace in our hearts and shedding it abroad, they will say, "That man is a child of God." Men do not believe in one man's talk, or in the other man's profession, but they do believe in a quiet holy endeavour to make and keep peace. It is easy to recognise this Godlike virtue of peace, because the world has so little of it. It shines like a star amid a stormy sky full of cloud-wrack. Christ, speaking of His peace, said, "Not as the world giveth, give I unto you."

There is no peace outside Christ, and directly peace really soaks into the Christian man's heart, and flashes through his life, and shines through his every movement, it is the most convincing proof that Christian people have got something the world cannot bestow or even imitate. They are *called* sons of God.

There is a time coming, and it cannot be far away, when all God's sons and daughters will be gathered to the Father's home and tread the courts of His palace. Let us try to imagine that the

present "little while" has vanished, and our Lord
has come, with all His saints, to His bridal feast?
See the regiments of His followers, as they pass—
First the poor in spirit, followed by the bands of
the meek, of them that mourn, of those that
hunger and thirst after righteousness. Here are
the merciful, and here the pure in heart, and here
the peacemakers. And as this last regiment
passes by, mark how the bright throngs of
spectators cry, "*These* are the sons of God, *they*
are likest God, *they* show His name written in
their foreheads."

There is nothing apparently in all the universe
so Godlike as this endeavour to make peace, not
by glozing over the surface, but by dealing with
those causes which underlie the quarrel and strife
of the world.

O God of Peace, grant me Thy Peace
unspeakable, that I may abound in Peace
through the power of the Holy Ghost.

IX

MARTYRS AND PROPHETS

*"Blessed are they which are persecuted for righteousness' sake : for theirs
is the kingdom of heaven,"* etc.—MATT. v. 10–12.

THIS beatitude completes the octave, but there
is no special reason why our Lord should
not have finished with the seventh, because the
eighth is altogether so different to the foregoing.
They rather deal with character, *this* with condition ; *they* with the internal quality of the
Christian soul, *this* with its external relation.
So far as we understand the first seven, they
might be developed in the spirit, apart from all
the world beside, immured in some secluded
grotto apart from the world ; but this indicates
that our Lord's conception for His Church

was that it would be constantly in the midst of the world; not of it, but in it; and therefore in perpetual collision and antagonism with its evil.

He seems to have been sketching His own life. These beatitudes tell the story of our Saviour's personal life, as, indeed, it is the story of His life as developed step by step in the believer's heart. They are therefore objectively and subjectively historical. They are *objectively* historical, for we know that our Lord Jesus was poor in spirit, emptied Himself, mourned and wept for the sin of man; was meek; hungered and thirsted for righteousness; was merciful and pure in heart; and that He came to make peace. All these qualities in our Saviour's experience brought Him to the Cross — brought him into collision with the evil of the world, and in three years to Calvary. Thus the beatitudes afford a true history of the progress of our Saviour's life from the emptying of the incarnation to the laying down of His life for men.

They are also true of each one of us. We begin by being poor in spirit, broken in heart, and lowly in mind. We pass through phase after phase of added knowledge of God and of His truth; and as we do so we approximate always more and more to the climax of the Cross, and just in proportion as we are like Christ in the attainment of these lovely qualities, we become like Him also in our suffering and sorrow even to death.

How clearly our Lord Jesus Christ predicts the effect which these qualities will have upon the world. It is as if He said, "It is impossible for you to be thus and thus without incurring a very avalanche of hate, but in the midst of it all, you may retain the blessed placidity and rest which I have promised. There is no need that the benedictions which I have already uttered to those who are merciful and meek and pure in heart, should forsake you when you stand at the stake or are nailed to the Cross, for the blessed life is altogether independent of outward circumstances; it may be deeply seated and rooted in the soul when all without is in turmoil and war."

One of the Scotch martyrs, when they were putting the faggots at his feet, said, " Methinks they are casting roses before me." Another of the martyrs, when he was about to die, said, "I was glad when they said to me, Let us go into the house of the Lord." And it is said of the great Argyle, that when his physician felt his pulse, as he laid his head upon the block, he could detect no fluttering, but the quiet steady beat of health and peace. Since, then, the qualities our Saviour characterised in the beatitudes were inevitably driving Him and all His followers into collision with the world, it was very delightful and beautiful of Him to say, "In the midst of all this you may be blessed; yea, you may rejoice, your heart may leap and bound with exceeding joy." And the more we think about it, the more sure it seems that all those who died for the faith had some special grace given which enabled them to be more than conquerors, and it will come still to those who are accounted worthy to suffer for Christ amongst men.

Let us notice, first, why we are persecuted; secondly, the manner of the persecution; thirdly, the blessedness which is possible amidst it all.

I. THE CAUSE OF PERSECUTION.

It is twofold. First we are "Persecuted for righteousness' sake," and then He says, "And shall persecute you for My sake." Evidently men must feel that His cause was righteousness; that He was the righteous Servant of God, and that righteousness was no longer an abstraction or sentiment, because He had embodied it. This is a great distinction, and makes it so much easier to suffer for Him. It is well enough to suffer for a cause, the cause of justice, truth, and righteousness, but how much better to think of suffering for Him! It is an inspiration to realise that righteousness is Christ, and that whenever men suffer for righteousness they do really suffer for Him who is the Prince of Righteousness and the King of Truth? Wherever there is right in the world for which men suffer, the cause of Jesus Christ is somehow implicated in it. But how wonderful that Jesus, at the very beginning of His ministry, a Nazarene peasant, standing amid a number of peasants on the Mount of Beatitudes, should identify the cause of righteousness with Himself in this marvellous combination. "For My sake," He said.

Now why is it that the world hates and persecutes us for His sake? There are just these reasons. *First,* that the more there is of Christ in us, the more we condemn the world, and there is nothing the ungodly man so dislikes as to have the search-light of unsullied purity flashed in upon the workings of his heart and life. Jesus Christ is to the ungodly what the sun at noontide is to the diseased eye; what the bounding joyousness of the child is to the weakened nerve. And hence it is in proportion as we are living in the power of Jesus Christ, and are bringing to bear the influence of our character and life upon other men that they wince beneath the impinging ray; they shrink from it; it causes them pain, and they turn naturally in indignant hatred on those who have thus inflicted upon them suffering.

Secondly, the more there is of Christ in us, the more we offend the pride of men and women around, who desire to have the admiration which we have, or which true godliness has, but which

they are not able to win, through their inability to
pay the price for it. Hence jealousy and envy
immediately begin to work. Remember how
Aristides was hated, because he was always called
"The Just." Men who were notoriously unjust
envied him the love of his fellow-citizens. And so
there will always be a great jealousy on the part
of the ungodly towards those who love Christ.

Thirdly, the Christ - spirit in any one of us is
always aggressive, and compels us to attack the
vested interests of wrong-doing. The Lord Jesus
never contemplated that His children should go
quietly through the world exerting only a negative
influence. He expected that there would be a
constant positive effect proceeding from His
Church, that, like salt, it would sting. But when
the craft is in danger, when the receipts fall off,
we naturally rouse the indignation of those who
suffer in consequence. The search-light brought
to bear upon the diseased conscience, the constant
feeling that the Christian possesses a character
which the ungodly cannot emulate, and which
wins an admiration they cannot receive, together
with the fear that worldly position and possessions are threatened by the progress of the

Christ-spirit — all these things tend to make men hate us.

And yet the source of hatred really lies deeper than all this. It seems as if there is a malignancy of hatred in evil against the good which cannot be perfectly explained by any of these reasons, and which must be attributed to that eternal war and hatred which exist between Satan and all his legions, and Jesus Christ and the armies of heaven. There is a great war in the universe, a fire raging beyond the range of our sight, and we may be pretty sure the signs of it will break out whenever we manifest on earth something of the purity and beauty of Jesus Christ our Lord. These are the causes of persecution.

II. THE FORMS WHICH THIS PERSECUTION TAKES.

Our Lord characterises it in three distinct ways —first, in word; secondly, in act; and thirdly, in imputation of evil. In word men reproach us; in act they persecute us; in imputation of evil they "say all manner of evil against us falsely for His sake." We need hardly dwell upon this. We

know something of the hiss of the serpent. We
have all suffered more or less from the unkind
word. We know what it is for stories to pass
round and round, for we ourselves have been only
too prone to take them upon our lips and pass
them forward. The word and the act, how many
have suffered, how many are suffering? Think of
the eight hundred Quakers—to take one of the
smallest religious sects — who in the reign of
Charles ii. suffered for their religion, and the one
million pounds exacted from that body in payment
of fines for conscience' sake, and of all the countless numbers who have suffered for the cause of
Christ.

And then as to the imputation of evil. I do not
think any of us should shrink from it. We are
very anxious about our character, but if we live
close to Christ, men will impute to us all manner
of evil. They will impugn our motives, mis-
represent our actions, and circulate malicious
stories about us. The nearer we live to Christ the
more certain it is it will be so; that if they called
Him Beelzebub they will call us the same. My
belief is that we should be very careless about
these things, and that the only time when we

should defend our character should be when
aspersions on it may injure the cause of Christ;
that as far as we are concerned we should be
content to lose our character and be counted the
off-scouring of all things.

When these reports are circulating, and these
stories being told, and these unkind words being
hurled from lip to lip, we should immediately turn
to our Master and tell Him we are content to
suffer with and for Him. Ask Him to intercede
for and to vindicate us, if it is His will we should
be vindicated, and if not, to give us grace to suffer
patiently and wait. We are so eager to stand
well; we are so sorry if the least thing is said
against us; we are so irritated if we are misunderstood and misrepresented; we are so anxious to
write the explanatory letter to the paper or the
private individual. It is a profound mistake. We
should be content to trust God with the aspersion,
to leave to Him our vindication, and meanwhile
to plod on, doing our work quietly day by day, as
in His sight, only being more tender and thoughtful and careful of those who have done us wrong.
That is the true Christian spirit.

III. The Beatitude.

Why is it that we are blessed, and how does the blessedness come? The Master says that they which are persecuted for righteousness' sake have the kingdom, and that was the very promise with which He commenced this series of Beatitudes, "Blessed are the poor in spirit, for theirs is the kingdom of heaven." It would almost seem, therefore, as if we had come back to where we started, but it is not quite so. It is quite true that the poor in spirit have the kingdom, and that those who are persecuted have the kingdom, but we must remember that just as steps in the spiral staircase always come back upon their starting-point, but upon a higher level, so we come back to the kingdom, but upon a higher level than we were when we started with the poor in spirit, and it may be that this series is constantly repeating itself in higher rounds. It may be that we shall begin to-day, by poverty of spirit, to climb up the spiral staircase towards this eighth beatitude, and then starting again from this eighth beatitude we shall pass, so to speak, through a higher series, passing through the same notes but in another key. We shall never get away from mourning, only we shall mourn for deeper reasons. We shall never cease to be learning the lesson of meekness, but it will be a deeper down meekness than ever before, one that dyes our very heart fibre. We shall always be seeking purity, but we shall have new conceptions of purity, and as we know these things in a more perfect degree we shall be persecuted more, and so every time we will come back and back and back to where we started, but higher up. Persecuted for righteousness' sake and yet possessing the kingdom.

Our Lord Jesus Christ was looking over the wall of time; there were patent to Him things which none but He knew of. In the tenth verse He speaks in the past tense, but in the present tense in the eleventh verse. "Blessed are they that have been persecuted for righteousness' sake, for theirs is the kingdom of heaven," as if at that moment He saw all the spiritual witnesses to the truth of God who had suffered from the time of Abel, and He says, "I see them, and they have already entered upon the royalties of the eternal world, and sit on thrones and judge"; and then turning to His disciples He said, "Blessed are ye when men shall revile you : for your reward is great in heaven." In future, when we are persecuted, I think it will help us if we seek to look into the future, as Jesus did, and realise the greatness of our reward, for every reward that we receive in heaven will carry with it greater opportunity of blessing in the ages that are yet to be. That was why the Lord spoke about thrones. The thrones on which we are to sit imply that we shall be able more widely to help those needing help ; to serve God more efficiently ; to minister before Him, and carry His blessed gospel, perhaps to regions of the universe where it has never been heard. We shall indeed be blessed if the persecution of this world shall make us more fit to serve and minister in the next.

Notice how the Lord Jesus puts the martyr upon the same footing as the prophet. He said, " So persecuted they the prophets," as if the martyr were a prophet. It is a profound thought, but a very true and deep one. The prophet stood among his fellows witnessing to the unseen and eternal ; the martyr or the sufferer does the same. So that the fagots on which the martyrs of Christ have been burnt have lighted up the souls of men almost as

9

much as the words of prophets have done, and have cast a glow upon the centuries. Prophets witness to the unseen and eternal by their words, sufferers do it by their agonies. If we, day by day, are willing to suffer for Christ in the workshop or in the home, we are drawing aside the veil of the unseen and eternal, through our fiery trials people are catching a glimpse of the faith and heroism and strength of Christianity, and we are witnessing to the reality of things unseen by ordinary vision, but which animate us to endure.

To Thee, my God, I flee, to hide from the rebuke and hate of man, who daily pursues, oppresses, and wrests my words; hide me in the secret of Thy pavilion, I entreat Thee, from the strife of tongues.

X

THROUGH THE GATES

"Blessed are they that wash their robes, that they may have right to the tree of life, and may enter in through the gates into the city."
—Rev xxii. 14 (R.V.).

THIS has been truly called the last beatitude of the ascended Christ. It is characteristic of our dear Lord that, as He had shown us the way of Blessedness from the Mount on which He taught His disciples, so He should complete the cycle by this last crowning and significant benediction, which embraces certain conceptions that could not have been presented, because they would not have been understood, until the Cross had been borne, and the Blood shed.

It is interesting to note the very great alteration which the R.V. makes in the text, therein following

the most approved ancient MSS. Formerly the
words read thus : *Blessed are they that do His commandments* ; and though it was clear that it would
be impossible to do so, apart from His grace
who bought us by His blood, and now waits to
succour us by His Spirit—yet the stress of the
verse was evidently on that obedience to command-
ment which savoured strongly of the old covenant.
To make entrance into the City of God depend
primarily on obedience, was not perhaps what we
might have expected, after all that is said in the
Epistles about our absolute indebtedness for all to
the unsearchable riches of God's grace.   Of course
such obedience is due to the operation of God's
grace ; of course, also, the work of God in the soul
can only be attested and vindicated by its effect on
our outward life ; but we must feel that there is
greater propriety in this final stress being laid on
the redemption which was purchased for us by the
Blood of the Cross.   There seems a fitness in this
emphatic reference to what Christ has done for us
on the Cross, as distinguished from what we are
called upon to do for Him.

I. The Homogeneousness of our Saviour's Life.

The angels that stood beside the little group which gathered on the Ascension Mount, said emphatically : *This same Jesus, which is taken up from you into Heaven, shall so come, in like manner.* Evidently they had no thought that the passage of the centuries, less or more, would alter Him in one trait of His character, or in one aspect of holy helpfulness to the sons of men.   However long the interval between His departure and return, however important the events that might transpire in the meanwhile, however lofty the dignity to which He might be exalted, He would always be the same Jesus—the same yesterday, to-day, and forever.

Some years ago I was privileged to make the friendship of a distinguished Indian missionary who, out of his intense devotion to the country which he had adopted for his Master's sake, wore the native dress, ate the native food, and even sat in the native fashion.   On his return to England on furlough, he still maintained these customs ; and on my remonstrating with him, and suggesting

that what might be suitable for India was un-
necessary in England, he replied : " If I were to
alter my style of living on my return to England,
the natives might suppose that I had only put on
the appearance of likeness to themselves, whereas
I wish them to realise that for the love of Christ I
have actually identified myself with their interests,
and have become an Indian."

This will assist us to realise how close is Christ's
identification with us. His Incarnation is not a
semblance merely, like the robes of light in which
He girds Himself. He has become one with us in
a very real and literal fashion, and now that He
has passed from our view He is not less the Son
of man because He is the acknowledged Son of
the Highest ; and He pursues the same course of
thought, action, and ministry, as when He sojourned
on our earth, sat on the mountain, walked beside
the lake, or floated across its heaving bosom.

What an illustration of this fact is presented
here ! He was sent to bless (Acts iii. 26). When
He opened His mouth and taught, He said, Blessed,
blessed, blessed (Matt. v. 3, etc.). His hands
dropped with the spices of blessing when He

placed them on the latch of men's hearts. Never
was He happier than when He wove some benediction into His ordinary talk (Luke vii. 23). He
blessed the food men eat, and transformed a
common meal into a sacrament. He was in the
act of blessing with outspread hands, when He
was severed from those who loved Him, and borne
upwards to heaven (Luke xxiv. 50, 51). The last
view men caught of our Saviour's person, was in
the act of blessing, with outstretched hands, as
when the priest came out of the temple and blessed
the waiting congregation. It is in harmony, therefore, with all we know of Jesus, to find Him utter-
ing such a benediction as this; and it is also in
conformity with what He tells us will be His
greeting to those who have faithfully obeyed
and imitated Him: "Come, ye blessed of My
Father."

Wherefore let us doubt not, but steadfastly
believe, that this same Jesus is the same loving
Saviour who, in the days of His flesh, so lovingly
blessed all who came to Him, and who, from His
throne in the glory, still stoops over our lives, with
His hands full, pressed down and running over

with the blessings which He desires to pour into
our lives, making us most blessed for ever, and
filling us with joy by His countenance.

II. The Force of this Metaphor.

"*Blessed are they that wash their robes.*"—This
book is dominated by Hebrew methods of thought,
and in the robe we must detect an allusion to
character, which is to the soul what our clothes
are to the body. Character is the robe in which
the inner man arrays himself. Indeed the word
"habit" (and character is just the collection of our
habits) is used alike of the material dress, and of
the inner and moral life. When Joshua is described
as standing before the Angel, clothed in filthy
garments, and when the prodigal returns to his
father in rags, we can but understand that their
character is reflected in the condition of their
dress: and that each is far removed from the
purity of heart and behaviour without which none
can see the Lord.

By nature the robe of our souls is splashed and
foul. "All our righteousnesses," the prophet says,

"are as filthy rags." And if our righteousnesses
are such, what must not our wickednesses be!
Not that all have gone to the same excess of riot,
nor have dyed their robes to an equal degree of
blackness; but that there is only One of the sons
of Adam that has escaped some spot or stain or
wrinkle. The Lamb was without blemish, and
without spot: all else need to wash their robes of
some pollution that has left its finger-mark upon
them. The meek were not always meek; the
pure not always chaste; the poor in spirit not
always humble; and if it were not for the
fountain opened for sin and uncleanness, the
cleanliness of God's Home were for ever an
inaccessible ideal.

But, as this book so constantly tells us, there
is a glorious possibility of becoming cleansed.
"These," says the Seer, "have washed their robes
and made them white in the Blood of the Lamb."
And if *they* succeeded in this, *we* may, so long as
"the Blood of Jesus Christ, God's Son, cleanseth
from all sin."

1. Be willing that the Holy Spirit should have
entire control of the deepest springs of thought

and motive, so that never again you may harbour the least thing that may grieve Him who bought you by His blood to be wholly His. Dwell much on His infinite and ineffable claims; and beware lest you count the blood by which you have been redeemed an unholy thing.

2. Spend much time in meditation upon that supreme act of the Divine Substitute, in virtue of which He died in the likeness of sinful flesh, that our old man should be annulled and brought to nought, that we should no longer serve sin. And let the cross put a finality to your subjection beneath the reign of evil habit and desire. "In that He died, He died unto sin *once* . . . likewise reckon ye also yourselves to be dead indeed unto sin."

3. Ponder much the tenderness of Him who died on the Cross, and is now exalted to be a Prince and a Saviour; His great horror of sin; its cost to Him, and His ability to deliver the soul that trusts in Him from the tyrant evils that have too long devastated it. Thus a great hatred of sin will become your second nature, and that blessed penitence and compunction will be yours,

which shall dissolve you in floods of penitential grief.

4. Remember, too, what Dr. Chalmers called the expulsive power of a new affection, and ask that the love of Jesus, as evidenced in His cross, may so constrain you that you may no longer live to yourself, but to Him who died and rose again.

5. Above all plead that promise of His, which so well embraces our deepest desires, and answers them: "Then will I sprinkle clean water upon you, and ye shall be clean: from all your filthiness, and from all your idols, will I cleanse you; I will put My Spirit within you, and cause you to walk in My ways." Let us claim that God would fulfil in us whatever He may mean by those great words. Oh to live under the shelter of the Cross, beneath the flow of the cleansing blood, in fellowship with Him who came by water and blood—not by water only, but by water and blood!

The Greek word might bear the force: *Blessed are they that are washing their robes.* That we have been washed once is not enough; we must go again and again to the Fountain opened for sin and uncleanness. Whenever we are conscious of

the least defilement, and before it can breed and
spread; whenever conscience accuses us; whenever
we have lost our place and feel out of fellowship
with God—we must get back again to the Laver,
just at the entrance of the Holy Place.

Oh souls of men, defiled and unfit for God's
pure eye, will ye not seek the pardon and salvation
which emanate from the Cross, and are to be
received by faith, that ye too may have the right
to the tree of life, and enter in through the gates
into the city?

III. THE RESULTS THAT WILL ACCRUE.

"*Right to the tree of life.*"—On the last page of
the Bible, we meet with the tree of life, from
which in the first pages we are told that man was
warned away. But here the restrictions are
removed. The Cherubim with flaming sword are
withdrawn. God Himself gives us a right to
come, and invites to eat abundantly of its precious
fruit.

Why is this? Why may we take that from
which our first parents were debarred? The

answer is not far to seek. We have been redeemed by the precious blood from the consequences of our transgression. The proud spirit of independence and isolation from God has been replaced by a tender, humble, renewed spirit. Life will not now be spent in the energy of the self-principle, but in living dependence on the true Vine ; therefore the Life, which is life indeed, is the glad requisite and possession of the cleansed soul. It has become one of those sheep that hear the Shepherd's voice, and of whom He said : I give unto them eternal life ; I am come that they might have life more abundantly.

Right to enter in through the gates into the city.— Excluded from the garden at the beginning, man is welcomed to the city which hath foundations, when the mystery of redemption, of sin and sorrow, is complete. The garden stands for solitude, comparative sluggishness, and evanescence; the city for society, activity, and permanence. Who will not be glad to reach that city, and enter its gates ! Like those of Peter's prison, they will open to us of their own accord ! And best of all, we shall have no perturbation or anxiety lest

our presence there should be challenged.   Pointing
to the Blood which has cleansed us, we may insist
on our *right* to be there, through the Blood of the
Cross which has blotted out the handwriting that
was against us, and opened to us a fellowship,
which death cannot annul, with the great multitude
of the saints.

O God, I humbly ask, that when Thou
callest me from this world of sin and sorrow,
Thou wouldest grant me an abundant entrance
to Thy kingdom and glory, through the Blood
of Jesus Christ, Thy Son.

PRINTED BY MORRISON AND GIBB LIMITED, EDINBURGH

BOOKS FOR THE HEART.

Edited, with an Introduction, by ALEXANDER SMELLIE, M.A.

Fcap. 8vo, printed on antique wove paper, cloth boards, gilt top, price 2s. 6d.

Volumes just added to the Series.

THE
RELIGIOUS AFFECTIONS.

By JONATHAN EDWARDS.

◆　◆　◆

THE JOURNAL OF
JOHN WOOLMAN.

With an Appreciation by
JOHN GREENLEAF WHITTIER.

"The Journal is quaint reading, and the language is charmingly piquant."—*Bookman.*

"'Woolman's Journal' was a remarkable book, and was a favourite with Charles Lamb, yet we doubt if it is much read in this country, and this neglect is a thing to be regretted."—*Athenæum.*

PUBLISHED BY
ANDREW MELROSE,
16 PILGRIM STREET, LONDON, E.C.

BOOKS FOR THE HEART.

Other Volumes in the Series.

GRACE ABOUNDING TO THE CHIEF OF SINNERS.

By JOHN BUNYAN.

Dr. WHYTE, Author of "Bunyan Characters," says: "My best thanks for your beautiful 'Grace Abounding.' Go on with such good work."

THE CONFESSIONS OF ST. AUGUSTINE.

Second Edition.

"No cheap edition of 'The Confessions' that we know of can at all compare with it in beauty of outward form. Type, paper, and binding are also irreproachable."—*Church Times*.

QUIET HOURS.

By JOHN PULSFORD, D.D.

Second Edition.

"It is essentially a volume for thoughtful men and women of reverent mind, and to them the pages often conned will be ever fresh."—*Rock*.

PUBLISHED BY
ANDREW MELROSE,
16 PILGRIM STREET, LONDON, E.C.